CAPTIVITY OF THE OATMAN GIRLS

The Extraordinary History of the Young Sisters Who Were Abducted by Native Americans in the 1850s American Wild West

WORLD CHANGING HISTORY

been derived from various sources. Please consult a licensed professional before attempting any techniques outlined in this book.

By reading this document, the reader agrees that under no circumstances is the author responsible for any losses, direct or indirect, that are incurred as a result of the use of information contained within this document, including, but not limited to, errors, omissions, or inaccuracies.

Table of Contents

INTRODUCTION

～

When you read about the Wild West, it sometimes becomes hard to separate fact from fiction. In movies, comics, magazines, and many books, the Wild West had been turned into a myth about epic shootouts and relentless gangs fighting against hardened deputies with gigantic mustaches. There is always a grain of truth in fiction, though. The Wild West did have its share of lawlessness, and it was nothing like the USA you know today. But how wild exactly was it? Did people really walk around with guns dangling from their holsters and rifles on their horses? Could you shoot anyone you had a disagreement with over a poker game? Were Indian raids as common as we see in movies? Were things truly that insane?

Well, not to that extent. Much of what you see in movies about the Wild West is dramatized, and it does make for good drama. The reality, however, was a little bit less wild than what has been portrayed to us over the years. It is said that tales surrounding that era of US history have been dramatized and mythologized even before the era ended! On the one hand, you had the legend of cowboys and gunslingers, living life on the edge and by their rules. They answered to no one and did whatever they wanted without ever succumbing to the will of 'the man.' In short, they represented freedom to many, even toward the later years of that era. On the other hand, you had the tough lawmen who were the image of justice, enforcing it by steel and powder and inflicting equal carnage about the lawless gunslingers as the latter did on the public.

Also known as the American frontier or Old West, this era simply represents the history and folklore, as well as culture, often associated with American expansion from the mid-nineteenth century to the early twentieth (1850 to 1924). The origins of this image can be traced to an even earlier period, all the way back to the early seventeenth century, when the American frontier expansion originally started. The period that had been highly popular and often dramatized, however, is that from the 1850s to the later 1910s. In most media, you will find extremely romanticized versions of the Wild West where freedom was tangible, and the law was optional.

In reality, though, the Old West was not entirely unlike American cities today in terms of violence and crime rates, at least. According to several historians, the theories and assumptions about the level of violence of the American Frontier were mostly hypothesized rather than actually proven. In other words, many older historians assumed that the Old West was violent and lawlessness prevailed, and they worked based on that assumption without much evidence supporting such claims. In fact, some historians claim that it was fairly civilized. Historian Eugene Hollon even went as far as to claim that the Wild West "*was a far more civilized, more peaceful, and safer place than American society today.*"

Yet, despite these claims and several historians claiming that the violence in the American frontier was exaggerated, this era in time still had its fair share of chaos and violence. This violence, however, exploded toward the latter half of the nineteenth century due to the US government's policy toward Native Americans (Plain Indians). Contrary to popular belief, things were not always crazy between Plain Indians and European settlers. In fact, in earlier times, relationships enjoyed extended periods of relative peace, as shown by several documented events such as the Indians helping with the Pilgrimage–they even celebrated the first

Thanksgiving with the settlers. There were also several trade deals between Indians and European settlers rather than violence and chaos.

This book is about the captivity of the Oatman girls and everything that occurred during their captivity and after. However, it is only right to understand the tensions that already existed between settlers and the Native Americans during those times. Many may argue about the cause of such a horrific act of violence, but if there is one thing history has proven, it is that there's more to a story than the events. So, before going into the details of the horrific deaths of the Oatman family, let's take a little walk down some of the most horrendous events that led up to our story.

CHAPTER ONE

⮕

A Little History

Tensions always existed between the natives and those who came to pillage their wealth. The Indians, though, quickly realized that they were outmatched. The colonials poured into their lands in great numbers, and they possessed superior knowledge and technology at that time. Back then, the only weapons that the Plain Indians knew were bows, clubs, and tomahawks. They could still cause damage, though, and they did clash with the early settlers on many occasions. This is why peace was preferred in those earlier centuries. The white settlers knew they would need the natives' help if they ever truly wanted to settle in the land.

During those days, Europeans acknowledged the Indians' right to their own lands and that they should retain ownership of their possessions. The Europeans were also smart enough to know that peace and keeping things friendly with the Indians was the best approach to move forward in these new circumstances. This is why the trade was quite profitable for both parties, especially the fur trade, which boomed during the early settlement relations. Looking back at those earlier times, you would find that trade and friendly relations with the Indians were quite common. Violence and conflict ensued quite often, but peace was always on the table, during the 16th, 17th, and early 18th century, at least. The settlers' strategy toward the native Indians started changing later, and trying to maintain peaceful relations was no longer their primary concern.

Still, that is not to say that terrible bloodshed did not occur in the 1600s and 1700s. Battles and wars often did erupt. These two centuries were the golden age for expansion, and colonials from all over Europe were arriving in the new world. With their incessant expansion, clashes ensued with the Indians. The Powhatan wars, for example, carried a high death toll on both sides, and there were consistent raids from both the whites and the Indians. However, the settlers did not really care about peace with the Powhatan. At some point during the Powhatan wars, which we will explore later in the book (there were 3), the Indians tried taking the legal course, and they sued for peace in 1623. The colonist forces claimed to have been willing to accept such peace, and they invited the Indians for peace talks.

The colonists, however, had no intention of peaceful negotiations. In the summit, they poisoned the wine and killed around 200 unsuspecting Indians. They then physically attacked and killed another 50 or so. While this incident was a response to a massacre committed by the Indians the year before, it does go to show how violent conflict could get and how often blood was spilled on both sides.

Sometimes, the whites' actions bordered on genocide, as with the case of the Kalinago Genocide of 1626. The leader of the Kalinago, Tegremond, had grown weary of the settlers' expansion efforts and their disregard for the indigenous people and their rights. The French and English settlers roamed freely in St. Kitts., taking the land that they wanted at will. Confrontations would often erupt between the Indians and the settlers, but Tegremond had had enough with the fighting. He hatched a plan to attack the white settlers and eliminate them, along with any indigenous groups that were helping them. The plot was betrayed when a woman called Barbe revealed it to the French and English settlers.

In retaliation, a joint coalition planned a vicious scheme of their own. They invited the Kalinago Indians to a party where they intoxicated them with alcohol. Then, after the Indians returned to their village, the attack happened. Around 120 Kalinago were slaughtered in their sleep, including the tribe leader Tegremond. The next day, thousands more were rounded up and taken to Bloody Point. Historians estimate that 2,000 Kalinago Indians were slaughtered, even after surrendering to the French and English. While some Kalinago barely managed to escape, their survival did not last long. By 1640, the remaining members of that tribe were all taken as slaves and shipped to Dominica—slave trade was quite common back then, and while the whites often relied on African slaves, with their advent to the new world, they began targeting Plain Indians to sell as slaves.

Another infamous incident is the Mystic massacre of 1637. Things were already tense between the Pequot and the English, who fought a war from 1637 to 1638. One of the horrible facts concerning this massacre was that it included native Indians in the attack. The Pequots were the most significant and dominant tribe in southeastern Connecticut, which was one of the earliest English colonies. There were always tensions between the Pequots and the Mohegan and Narragansett tribes. While things were relatively peaceful for a while, when the European colonists established trade with all three tribes, the peace did not last for long. Eventually, the Pequots became allies with the Dutch colonists, while the other two tribes became allies with the English.

With these allegiances shifting the underlying currents of relations in the area, tensions arose, and soon, raids began on both sides. It was a particular raid by the Pequots that caused things to escalate when 200 warriors raided a colony and ended up killing 9 civilians, including 3 women. The Pequots demanded retribution, and it came swiftly. You need to understand that calls for wars with the Indians were quite common back then. Whenever the natives raided a colony or attacked settlers, there would always be someone calling for war and violent retaliations, which often happened, as with this case.

The Connecticut towns rallied together and started assembling a war party. They eventually gathered a force of 90 white men and 70 Indians from the Mohegan and Narragansett tribes, led by Captain John Mason. The colonial forces then commenced their attack on the night of May 26, 1637. They surrounded a Pequot village and closed off all exits. They tried to force their way inside, but the Pequots were ready, and they put up a fight.

This was when an order was given to set the entire village on fire and barricade the two exits. The Pequots were trapped inside the smoldering village. Many tried to escape by climbing the walls and barricades, but they were shot by the colonial forces. Those who managed to escape the gunfire and blazing fires were slaughtered by the Narragansett warriors. It is said that only five Pequots managed to escape, and a few were taken as prisoners. This is considered by many to be the first total war by colonist forces in the new world, and it was a horrible massacre. Accounts of that day live in infamy to this day, and tales of the Mohegans scalping each fallen Pequot are many. Even the colonist stories speak of how horrible the attack was. Captain John Underhill had joined forces with Mason, bringing along 20 more men for the attack. These were his words on the attack on the Pequot village:

"Captaine Mason entring into a Wigwam, brought out a fire-brand, after he had wounded many in the house, then he set fire on the West-side where he entred, my selfe set fire on the South end with a traine of Powder, the fires of both meeting in the center of the Fort blazed most terribly, and burnt all in the space of halfe an houre; many couragious fellows were unwilling to come out, and fought most desperately through the Palisadoes, so as they were scorched and burnt with the

very flame, and were deprived of their armes, in regard the fire burnt their very bowstrings, and so perished valiantly: mercy they did deserve for their valour, could we have had opportunitie to have bestowed it; many were burnt in the Fort, both men, women, and children, others forced out, and came in troopes to the Indians, twentie, and thirtie at a time, which our soldiers received and entertained with the point of the sword; downe fell men, women, and children, those that scaped us, fell into the hands of the Indians, that were in the reere of us; it is reported by themselves, that there were about foure hundred soules in this Fort, and not above five of them escaped out of our hands."

It is estimated that 400 to 600 Pequots died that day, including women, children, and elders. Later accounts report that Captain Underhill justified the murder of such innocents by, "*sometimes the Scripture declareth women and children must perish with their parents... We had sufficient light from the Word of God for our proceedings.*" This massacre is considered by many to be a genocide in the literal sense, not only because of the massive number of casualties but also because of what happened in its wake. The Pequots' spirits were broken by this massacre, and their will to fight was extinguished. Another battle took place between the

Pequots and their enemies not long after, and they suffered great losses then too.

After such heavy blows, the Pequots were no longer a tribe. A peace treaty required the surviving Pequots to be integrated into the Mohegan and Narragansett, and they had to stop referring to themselves as Pequots. This is a prime example of a massacre against an indigenous tribe that left few of them alive, and those surviving few were banned from claiming their heritage and identifying themselves as Pequots.

The Pound Ridge massacre was similar to the Pequot's in terms of its brutality and its disregard for all the rules of war and fair conduct. It was a part of the Kieft's War, which took place between the Lenape Indians and the colony of New Amsterdam. The war was over the same reasons that have been repeated over the years. Disputes broke out over lands, livestock, and taxation, which was being newly enforced on the Indians in the region. As tensions arose, this massacre was committed in retaliation to attacks by the Indians, and as always, the response was disproportionate and extremely violent. This incident also featured Captain John Underhill, who led a force of New Netherland soldiers on an attack on a Wappinger Confederacy village. The attack also began at night.

Ironically, the village they attacked was called Nanichiestawack, which translates to 'place of safety,' but it would not be one on that March 1644 night. The Lenape were gathered in a social ceremony that night on sacred lands, and they had guests from other local tribes as well. While historians differ on the exact spot of the attack, we know that it happened during this winter ceremony. Under a full moon, the colonial forces attacked. The surprise was sufficient to lead to the deaths of around 200 Indians before they could properly react. There was no escape, just like the previous massacre. The attackers had barricaded all exits and made sure that no one was leaving.

Some Lenape barricaded themselves in their homes and tried firing arrows at the attacking colonials. As with the previous attack, John Underhill ordered the houses burned with the people in them. It is reported that it was mostly women, children, and elders barricaded inside the houses, but that did not matter to the colonials. "*What was most wonderful is that among this vast collection of Men, Women, and Children, not one was heard to cry or to scream,*" said Underhill of that attack. The violent attack left over 600 Indians dead at the very least. What makes this attack even worse, was the fact that the Indians thought they were safe on their sacred lands, protected by peace treaties with the colonials, treaties that Underhill and his men blatantly violated.

It should come as a surprise that statues commemorating people like John Mason have been erected and are still around to this very day. We're talking about mass murders who killed women and children without batting an eye and who were celebrated often and considered as heroes among generations. Mason's statue was smeared several times, and several civil rights movements demanded its removal, especially during the USA's Black Lives Matter movement in 2020. However, the statue still stands as a testament to what the country thinks of people like John Mason.

Delving back into white-Indian relations, this was the setting into which the Wild West was born. There was peace at times and carnage at many other times. There were those who upheld the peace and wished to keep friendly relations with the Indians, but they were always outnumbered by people with had no regard for human life. As the years went by, things gradually became much worse for Plain Indians. The Europeans tried to keep the peace at some point during the first few centuries of their colonization; this much was a fact. Looking back on those times, it is documented that by the 20th century, almost $800 million were paid for Indian territories and lands. This goes to show that trade was the way to go in many cases, though there were still tensions and wars, especially when white settlers would go back on deals made and not pay the Indians, or when the indigenous people would attack settlers or vice versa.

Things, however, were about to change by the end of the American Civil War (War between States). This marked the transition from militias to a standing army. With this transition, it became apparent to the powers that there was a cheaper way to acquire lands from Indians: violence. As such, the European settlers and railroad companies began using the US army to steal lands from the Indians. This is where the relationships between white European and native Indians turned from peaceful trading to continuous raiding, and violence replaced friendly relationships.

The Americans had decided that it was exhausting and futile to try and keep the Indians pleased all the time. It was just easier to wipe out any who stood in their path and in the path of the railroads. This narrative was supported across the entire country, especially after decades of white-Indian violence and abductions. Many of the settlers had had enough, and they already had the view that the Indians were savages. So, enforcing their will upon the native inhabitants of the land by force of arms was no longer a murky issue or an unethical dilemma. It was something that needed to be done.

We are not talking about individual incidents. It was about the US army attacking whole Indian towns and villages. This was the general direction of the country, and it was even declared in legislation. Congress decreed in 1871 that no further treaties were to be ratified with Indians, making it official that there were no more intentions to peacefully negotiate deals that benefit both parties. Things were changing, and peaceful relations with the Indians were no longer on the table. American officials and soldiers were not shy about declaring their intentions toward Indians, too. Reading some of the announcements and statements from that time, one can only understand how the violence started. *"We are not going to let a few thieving, ragged Indians check and stop the progress of the railroads,"* says General William Tecumseh Sherman, who was given command of the Military District of Missouri. Sherman was given this command for the main purpose of waging war against the Plain Indians to make room for the railroad companies.

Considering the number of generals and (newly founded) Republican Party members that were invested in the railroad construction, clearing the Indians from the path of the railway network was of immense importance. It didn't stop at just displacing the Indians from their lands; some generals even suggested forcing the Indians to work on the railway construction to be overseen by Union army veterans. This would not have been new, considering the fact that settlers had been kidnapping Indians to be sold as slaves for the past few centuries. However, it was not something that the US government was interested in. This suggestion was rejected, and the US government opted to eradicate any Indians that got in the way. General Sherman is even quoted with the infamous term 'the final solution of the Indian problem,' which was to kill as many Plain Indians as possible and banish the rest from their lands. According to several historians, Sherman ordered his men to attack villages, particularly, in winter to kill as many men, women, and children as possible. Their livestock was also ordered to be destroyed so that the survivors would starve without any available sources of food—even their dogs were killed. Sherman is said to have regarded Plain Indians as "a less-than-human and savage race."

In short, General Sherman, as well as other generals in the US army and politicians, was not subtle or shy about declaring his intention to 'exterminate' Indians to make room for the 'racially superior white Americans and their culture of progress.' The terrible quote, "*the only good Indian is a dead Indian,*" is often attributed to General Philip Henry Sheridan, who also played a prominent role in the Indian wars. There are many documented cases of such genocidal intentions, like the Sand Creek Massacre, which happened in November of 1864. A Cheyenne and Arapaho village in Sand Creek, Southern Colorado, had Indians that were promised safety by the US government—they even had to hang a US flag over the village, which they begrudgingly did to be safe. It did not matter, though.

Colonel John Chivington was another civil war military commander whose role extended into the Indians wars. He raided that village with over 600 heavily armed soldiers with the sole intention of killing everyone in it. He is quoted saying, "*I want you to kill and scalp all, big and little; nits make lice.*" Estimates say that 163 Indians were killed on that bloody day, most of which were women and children. When he returned to his fort, Chivington and his men displayed their bounties: one hundred scalps. Those men were hailed as heroes even by newspapers, which claimed that those soldiers basked in "glory." The Indians weren't just killed. They were heavily mutilated and made to be an example for other Indians across the country.

"I saw the bodies of those lying there cut all to pieces, worse mutilated than any I ever saw before; the women cut all to pieces ... With knives; scalped; their brains knocked out; children two or three months old; all ages lying there, from sucking infants up to warriors ... By whom were they mutilated? By the United States troops," says John S. Smith in his congressional testimony.

Other testimonies from that attack are so gruesome and horrible; one could not help but shudder upon reading them. They include descriptions of killing pregnant women and children, as well as injured civilians who pleaded for their lives. No mercy was granted, though. This massacre was one of the worst committed by the American forces again Plain Indians, and it was all for land and wealth.

Yet, despite the story of this massacre and countless others by the European settlers, the biggest genocide committed by the settlers was not through force of artillery or weapons. It was by a disease.

The whites brought a myriad of diseases to the new world that killed millions of native Indians. The whites' expansion was done by the force of arms and their superior weaponry, true, but this was not the only reason. The whites' superior firearms could not account for the massive extinction rates among Plain Indians. It was, in fact, the diseases that they carried along from their original world that spread amongst the Indians like wildfire, killing many.

Experts estimate that 90-95% of the native population of the Americas had been killed within a few hundred years. This amounted to millions of natives who were died in the many waves of plagues and diseases. No matter how fearsome the settlers' weapons were, they could not account for this massive loss of life. Instead, the Europeans carried a weapon that they were not aware of - pathogens. The worst of these diseases is assumed to be Smallpox, which is a viral infection that travels to the victim's lungs and infects the lymphatic system. It only takes a few short days for significant pustules to spread across the patient's body, beginning with the hands and face. Worst of all, these blisters carry a highly infectious strand of Smallpox. If one gets punctured, it can infect all those surrounding the patient in close proximity.

Whether or not the infected survived Smallpox was a matter of chance. In total, the disease is incubated in the body for 12 days. During that time, if the patient is not quarantined (which did not often happen in the early days), they could infect dozens of people, who would, in turn, infect dozens of others. For the people of Europe, these diseases had been around for quite some time. Diseases like influenza, Smallpox, and measles had infected generation after generation, so there was some sort of immunity with certain groups of people. A lot of people used to die in these communities, yes, because antibiotics had not yet been invented. However, there were always those who survived an outbreak.

As for the Plain Indian communities, they sadly had no previous contact with these pathogens and germs. Due to the herding habits of the natives, there was little contact with a variety of animals that could infect them. So, cross-species infections were rare, if any, among the native Indians. This was about to end with the Europeans advent to the new world. They came carrying germs that have mutated over the span of generations and centuries. These germs and pathogens prospered in populated communities, and they found easy victims in the indigenous people, whose bodies were completely foreign and unprepared for such an attack. They had never experienced the flu, or measles, or any form of other diseases that the whites brought along. As a result, those infections ravaged the indigenous population, killing as many as 90-95% over the span of a few centuries.

It wasn't just the Americas that suffered the pathogens and diseases that white settlers brought along. European colonists also used this weapon to great effect in New Zealand, Australia, and African communities, rendering the communities and indigenous people unable to fight the colonization attempts.

With this brief background on the tensions and relations that marred this period in time, you start to understand where the violence in the American frontier stemmed from. As a result, the Plain Indians did not sit idly by and let their lands be ravaged, and their people be killed, be it by disease or weapon. They retaliated in kind, and they often committed crimes that were no less brutal than their adversaries, which created the violence that you often hear about in the 1800s and 1900s. These were times when any travel was too risky lest your party would be raided by the enemy, which happened too often. Settlers traveling in wagons or wagon trains were often left vulnerable to Plain Indian raiding parties or bandit attacks, and the bandits were not always plain Indians. In many cases, they were European settlers who took advantage of the fact that settlers would travel with their money, gold, and other valuable possessions.

Such highwaymen included the notorious Jack Powers, who continued to raid a long travel road in California until he was hunted by a band of vigilantes. Community justice was not uncommon then, and there was a degree of lawlessness, with each community practicing different sets of policing practices and with their own idea of law and order. They did not call each other 'cowboys,' though, because that was not a good label back then. If anything, it was derogatory and was often used to label criminals.

These were times when official law and order were not exactly common, which makes sense considering the ever-expanding landscape. It was not uncommon then for gangs to take the law into their hands. It is said that many were hanged to their death without trial or with mock trials that lasted a few minutes—sometimes, those hanged were Indians; others, it was alleged criminals. Justice was executed brutally, and those suspected of criminal wrongdoings were often hanged or shot. This was fairly common in the state of California, where crime rates had spiked after the gold rush (the discovery of gold in that area in the mid-19th century).

This was also the time when private agencies (such as Pinkerton National Detective Agency) acted as law enforcers and protected properties. Still, some areas or towns in the American frontier were notoriously known as outlaw towns where the law was not always enforced. As time passed, however, even those towns began establishing laws and putting some rules in place. Some towns, like Tombstone, started banning the carrying of firearms in plain sight to avoid scenes of people drinking at bars or playing poker games with guns dangling from their sides. There was the occasional gun duel, but those were few and far between and were less dramatized than in the movies, as we mentioned earlier. In most of those lawless duels, the winner would be arrested and presented to trial— though in some cases, the one who killed their opponent in a duel could be acquitted since it was a fair fight.

To sum up, before we delve into our story, the Old West was complicated. It did have its fair share of lawlessness, albeit not as grand or dramatic as the movies often show. Characters like Billy the Kid and Butch Cassidy were real, and they were notorious outlaws who lived lawless lives, but much liberty had been taken with dramatizing their stories and romanticizing their lives.

The root of much of the violence in the 18ᵗʰ and 19ᵗʰ centuries due to the American-Indian relations. Not all whites wanted to exterminate the Plains Indians as General Sherman, or his contemporaries did. There were times of peace between the two parties, though they were sometimes marred by conflict and raids. Many whites wanted the peace to endure with the Indians, but the government had the final say in how the Plain Indians were viewed and treated. In terms of labeling them, the government often dehumanized Plain Indians and labeled them 'wild beasts,' which did not help the situation. This was used as a justification to exile them and slaughter many of them. On the other hand, Canada was constructing its own transcontinental railroad without that kind of aggression and extermination against Indians, which is why many Plains Indians migrated to Canada to avoid being hunted by the US army.

As a result of these practices, tragedies such as the ones in this book happened. Violence ensued, and terrible crimes were committed on both sides, though it was obviously much more on the American side. The

American railroads could have been built without this much bloodshed and without the need to enslave many in reservations. Sadly, because a few men in power ordained it, countless lives were lost, and the American frontier witnessed brutal horrors that plagued it for many years.

CHAPTER TWO

⁓

The Journey West

Before we talk about the Oatman family, we need to understand the mindset of settlers. The Spanish are attributed as some of the earlier, if not the first, white settlers to arrive in North America. The Europeans started flocking to the new world for several reasons. They wanted to gain access to even bigger wealth, for starters, and the Americas had much of that. The white settlers also wanted to expand their influence over the world affair, and the Americas offered fertile ground for that. The European settlers generally had varying goals and expectations for the conquest of the new world. The Spanish, for instance, had one of three goals in mind: conquer, convert, or become rich. Christianity was at a high point at that time, and indoctrinating others was high on the clergy's list of important quests.

The Spanish even justified their conquest claims of the new world as a divine right and claimed they were helped by God himself in order to spread his message.

The settlers of Spain said it was their duty to save the native peoples of these lands from eternal damnation by inviting them to embrace Christianity. Over the next century, other European settlers, Portuguese and French, began claiming their rights in the new world, too, each with different goals in mind.

It was the English, though, that managed to establish a more permanent presence in the new world, establishing the first lasting colony in 1607. The first settlers of Jamestown came with hearts filled with greed. They were mostly rich nobles who did not want to farm crops or anything, which made those early years even more difficult. They just wanted to search for gold, and they found none. After some trying times and starvation, the settlers began understanding the importance of working and making an effort in order to survive.

Over the next few centuries, more settlers started flocking into the new world, which was tempting in more ways than one. For starters, the land was cheap, and it was easier to own lands in the new world than it was back in Europe. This promise tempted many settlers to travel to the Americas in order to own land and make a better life for themselves. The promise of religious freedom was also quite tempting for many people, and it plays an important factor in the story we are about to tell. The colonies promised people more freedom to practice their beliefs with more freedom than Europe, which was often plagued by religious persecution at that time. English and Dutch colonies, in particular, had more religious diversity. As a result, Roman Catholics, Anglicans, Calvinists, Puritans, Amish, and even Jews, among others, started escaping to the New World in the hopes that they could practice their beliefs freely and without persecution.

And thus, our story begins with Royce Oatman (sometimes spelled Royse). Royce was born in Vermont in the early 1800s to a family of Dutch immigrants. With the American expansion and all the changes that the society was going through, religion was often a controversial topic, and people switched faiths quite often, which was not uncommon or something to be surprised at. Royce's family was taken by the religious sentiments of that time and converted from the Dutch Reformed Church to Methodist. Many people were captivated by the evangelical wave that was sweeping across the country, including Royce's family.

Royce's family migrated across the country, which was also very common during these times of expansion, where settlers were discovering the magic of the country and the vast landscapes. The Oatman family explored farming opportunities in several areas, including Illinois, Indiana, and Ohio River Valley, in search of a better life. At the age of 23, Royce married Mary Ann Sperry, and they had seven children from 1834 to 1849. During that time, the family came in contact with the Mormon faith that would eventually change their lives for good.

Royce and his family met Joseph Smith, the Vermonter who declared himself a religious leader and a prophet of a new sect known as the Latter-Day Saints, which we know today as Mormons. To understand the background of the Oatman family and why they decided to migrate, we need to delve deeper into who Joseph Smith was and the impact he had on many people in that period of time.

It was believed that Smith could see things others could not see. He was said to use this spiritual insight (using crystal balls) to glimpse at mountains of silver and gold as well as ghosts. Leveraging his charisma, Smith took advantage of the religious fervor that was spreading across America in those days. Only aged 25, he published the Book of Mormon. This new gospel was translated, according to Smith, from golden plates that he found buried in a hill not far from his father's farm. According to those mystical plates, there was a group of white people called Nephites that are "delightsome" and Lamanites, who are dark and "loathsome" people. Those two groups supposedly fled Jerusalem in ancient times, around 600 BC, and settled in America.

The golden plates were kept hidden by Smith in a locked box, where he worked on 'translating them' using special glasses that were handed to him by the angel Moroni, who is the son of Mormon according to the Book of Mormon. While no one had ever seen it, Smith acquired testimonies from a handful of men that they had. Unsurprisingly, Smith's new religion caused massive controversy in several circles. A few dismissed his new calling as fraud, though they did not pay it much attention. Others, however, were outraged by his attempts to preach a new religion. What was most surprising, however, was that many people believed Smith's claims and flocked to join his new order and sought affiliation with the Latter Day Saints.

Naturally, things were not easy for the new prophet as well as his followers. In the chaos of it all, Smith claimed that he received a revelation. His congregation was to seek out the New Jerusalem or the city of Zion. Smith volunteered several of his followers (dubbed saints) to search for this new haven that was supposed to be the new home for his flock. Things quickly turned sour for this new religion, and people became hostile toward the Mormons. In the 1830s, Mormonism had spread in Ohio, but a social revolt arose against Smith and his followers. They were quickly branded as outcasts and were eventually driven out of the state. They were constantly harassed and picked on everywhere, and conflict brewed wherever they went. The Mormons eventually fled to Illinois to avoid persecution.

While the people of Illinois initially sympathized with this flock and its new faith, after everything they had been through, their sentiments quickly changed when they realized that the Mormon church believed in polygamy and even endorsed it. This went against the religious doctrine that was common back then. The Mormons eventually were unwelcomed in Illinois, too. Royce Oatman, however, was captivated by this new religion along with his family. They joined the church with the same zeal that fueled their earlier conversion to Methodism, dazzled by this new faith and everything it offered its believers.

The Mormons grew quite powerful in Illinois, and Smith's power was significant in his earlier years. He eventually became the mayor of Nauvoo, Illinois, and had significant political power. He even considered running for President. Things naturally did not sit well for the average person in Illinois. Many had flocked to Mormonism, abandoning traditional doctrine. This, along with the notion of polygamy that offended many, as well as Smith growing political influence, led to the Mormons becoming outcasts in Illinois as well. People started rising against the church's growing power and demanding that something is done to thwart the Mormon church's growing influence in Illinois.

Smith made a mistake that was the final straw when he closed down a newspaper that accused him of sexual misconduct and abusing women. When that happened, the government issued warrants to arrest Smith and his brother, Hyrum. Many in Illinois were already dreading Smith and his influence, fearing that he might one day declare himself King among men. Joseph and Hyrum surrendered to the authorities and were subsequently arrested along with some of Smith's followers. On June 27, 1844, an angry mob stormed the jail where the brothers were held and killed them both. Some say the mob was incited by the Masonic lodge who accused Smith of stealing Masonic secrets.

Five men were later arrested and tried for Smith's death, but they were all acquitted.

After his death and burial in Illinois, Smith was lauded as a religious fanatic who stirred people and incited wrongdoings by non-Mormon newspapers. For the Mormons, however, he was hailed as a martyr and a prophet who died as a punishment for his faith. Smith's death left a gaping void in the Mormon Church, and another leader needed to step up. Like many other Mormons, the Oatman's waited anxiously for a new leader to step up and fill the void that Smith left to guide the not-so-new faith, not any longer. While others have tried, James Colin Brewster is the one most relevant to our story.

Brewster was already notorious when he was just ten years old. Rumors spread that this young boy was special and could see visions and things that no other could see. Like Smith, Brewster was not educated, and there was an aura of mystery surrounding his so-called visions. This vagueness and mystical charisma, however, intrigued the elders of the Mormon Church. They took a look at Brewster and quickly declared him their new prophet, seer, and interpreter of religious texts. To no one's surprise, after being proclaimed the new prophet and seer, Brewster's visions became more frequent and specific.

Brewster claimed that he was visited by Moroni, the same angel that had visited Joseph Smith. He claimed this angel commanded him to write religious texts, which he wrote. Brewster could not read or write, so his father wrote them for him, taking dictation with the help of scribes. Brewster eventually claimed that there was a distant gathering point for all the loyal 'saints' of the Mormon church, without specifying where exactly. Brewster did not last long in the Mormon Church, testing their patience with his prophetic claims and so-called visions. He was quickly denounced by the Mormon Church after his ego got the better of him. The Mormons claimed he was straying away from Smith's teachings as only the latter was allowed to take the commandments from the angel. Brewster later went on to establish the Church of Christ.

Even with Brewster's expulsion from the church, the Mormons were in disarray. Despite his short tenure with the Mormons, Brewster had managed to amass a following, and some found him to be their next leader and savior. A war of words ensued between the self-dubbed Brewsterites and the rest of the Mormons. One of those who found Brewster to be the leader they were looking for was Royce Oatman.

The so-called promised land that Brewster spoke of was named the Land of Bashan, which was supposed to be somewhere toward Southwest America. So, Royce Oatman sold the family possessions in preparation for the pilgrimage. The family packed the few things they thought would be necessary for their new life, and they followed the other Brewsterites on a journey west in search of Bashan. The journey started in 1850 from Independence, Missouri. This small convoy was filled with the hope of finding a promised land where they would know peace and spiritual enlightenment. The journey, however, proved to be something else entirely.

It did not take long for conflict to arise amid the small convoy of some 50 to 90 something colonists. They initially took the Santa Fe Trail, which was anything but safe. Dissent, however, quickly spread among the hopeful followers. Some were not impressed with the Brewster family's leadership skills and their general vagueness. After all, the message that James Brewster claimed he had received did not exactly specify where Bashan would be, so there was no telling whether or not the caravan was headed toward this promised land or was just lost. Some eventually decided to split up and take a different route, disillusioned with Brewster's aimlessness. So, several of the wagons parted ways and followed a different path and followed Santa Fe Trail with all its perils.

Royce Oatman led a group of families that separated, and they took the Southern Route across Socorro and Tucson while the other Brewsterites took the Northern Route. Those who followed Brewster were in for a tough journey as the weather was dry and humid, and the road was unkind and unforgiving. Royce Oatman and the families with him had the goal of heading toward California, thus opted for the quicker Southern Route. Their journey was not much kinder than the Brewsterites, though. After assuming command of the company near Socorro, Oatman was relentless and without mercy. He led his party for long hours in rough terrains that none of them were quite accustomed to under the blistering sun—keep in mind that these were all families with many children tagging along.

The group soon delved into New Mexico Territory and quickly approached the dangers of Indian territory. The Brewsterites, and those who were fed up with their antics, split up near Santa Fe, taking different routes, as we mentioned earlier. Taking this Southern Route, the Oatman's and company crossed into a part of the country that the Mexicans had labeled "Jornada Del Muerto," which translates to 'Journey of Death.' The road became even more unfriendly, and they were met with several warning signs. Delving into the unknown, the convoy came across human bones, dead animals, and several other ominous signs that this road was not safe. The group naturally was stricken with fear, but they still plowed on.

It is said that a US government mail train crossed paths with the travelers and warned them that the area was swarming with Indians and they should leave. The group ignored him and moved forward, confident that they were under God's protection. The Oatman's were soon abandoned by some members of the wagon train who turned back to follow Brewster in October 1850. The presence of this convoy in Indian territory did not go unnoticed. The Plains Indians were aware of the trespassers, and they often sized them up. The Indians raided the caravan several times at night to steal some of the livestock, which was one of the factors that contributed to the tensions between the wagons and, eventually, led to that split in October 1850.

Losing several of their animals in such hostile territory did not make the ride any easier for the Oatmans and their companions. Unfortunately, things were not about to get any easier. The summers of 1850-1851 were some of the driest ever recorded in that era, which made survival for the naïve travelers even harder. It wasn't just them that struggled to survive the heat and dry weather, too. The Indians, too, tried to survive and were faced with similar complications in the extreme weather. It is reported that some of the oxen that traveled with the group would collapse in exhaustion, as did members of the company that followed Royce Oatman.

It was January of 1851 when the Oatman party reached Tucson, battered and exhausted from the arduous journey that spanned several months since their departure in mid-1850. By that time, Tucson was a Mexican town. The travelers were eager to purchase some food and supplies to replenish their depleted resources after months of traveling, not to mention undergoing several raids by the Indians along the road. To their bad luck, few supplies were available for them to purchase. The entire area was suffering from Apache raids, which left few supplies to offer. The group did not get the rest that they were hoping for, and so they moved along.

The Oatman party traveled around 'the Peak,' the mountain observation point used by several Indian tribes for centuries earlier. They reached a small but friendly Pima village. Desperate to resupply to continue on their journey, the Oatman's were as unfortunate as they had been in Tucson. They were informed by the Pimas that the little supplies that they had were not for sharing, because they too were constantly raided by the Apache, who left no supplies to share with weary travelers.

Looking back on this journey, one could only conclude that stopping for some rest or finding proper shelter for a few months was the right course of action. In New Mexico, now Arizona, the Oatman company was weary from their travels, and they had little supplies to sustain them, least of all take them to California, which was still a long journey. They had lost several animals along the way, mostly due to Indian raids but also to exhaustion. As if those warning signs, both plain and implied, were not enough, one of the women in the convoy gave birth. This was another indicator that the convoy should stop for a while, but Royce Oatman had another say. He insisted that the wagon train pushes on in search of Bashan.

Oatman said that Bashan was not far then, only a few hundred miles west of where they were. He insisted that the convoy moves ahead, which did not sit well with the other families. The parents who had just welcomed a new child to the world did not deem it a good idea to move forward in such trying circumstances, surrounded by danger from all sides. The other families as well opted to stay behind in a wise decision. They were not certain that they would find more supplies on the road, especially with the latest failed attempt with the Pimas. They also feared the possibility of attacks from the Indians if they were out in the wilderness on their own.

Tragically enough, Royce Oatman and his wife were also expecting another child to his already big family, supposedly arriving within three to four weeks. Oatman, however, had no intentions of sitting around doing nothing while waiting for the child to arrive. He stubbornly moved forward despite all the risks that awaited. He took his family with him, but they were all alone when they resumed their travels along the dangerous trail; the other families all lagged behind. Royce Oatman was obsessed with finding the holy city, and he decided to brave the road with his family without any protection.

In Oatman's defense, there were claims that the road up west toward California was safe. While staying with the Pimos, one Dr. Lecount arrived from Fort Yuma, where the wagon train was supposedly headed. Lecount was someone with vast experience in the Pacific Coast and had traveled plenty. He told them that the route was safe, and they had nothing to worry about. He said that he had not encountered hostile Indians, and his party was not raided on their journey from Fort Yuma, nor had they heard about such incidents. This naturally encouraged Oatman to move forward. One needs to understand the state of mind that Oatman, and his company, were in at that moment.

They feared overstaying their welcome with the Pimas, and the fact that there were little if any, supplies to share certainly did not help. They were also weighed by the grueling journey they had been on for the better part of a year, with the promise of their destination only a few hundred miles away. They had all heard great things about California, and getting there was something they all desired. While the other families decided to stay to avoid any problems along the road to Fort Yuma, Oatman was embarrassed to overstay his welcome and just wanted the journey to be over with. And so, the Oatman's moved ahead with their journey without the other families, carrying the few supplies they could obtain, which was far from enough for a few hundred miles' journeys.

Royce Oatman led his family along the Gila River, which flowed west. Their plan was to cross the river's southwest portion, which was a shortcut in a way. This shortcut meant that they would cover some hard terrain and travel in harsh conditions. A few days into their journey, the Oatman's were already starving. They did not have enough provisions to cover them for such an arduous journey. The few cattle they had left were also suffering, unable to drag the wagons with the family's belongings. The animals tripped and stumbled, unable to keep up with the steep climbs and the rough terrain, especially while starved and exhausted from their long travels.

In order for the oxen to handle such climbs, the wagons would have to be unloaded and then lifted, which was strenuous and exhausting. Unfortunately, this was not a one-time occurrence. One time after the other, the wagons were emptied and lifted and then reloaded once again. It wasn't just the wagons that needed to be lifted. Rocks and sand needed to be cleared from the way in order for the wagons' wheels to move smoothly. Needless to say, this was laborious work that quickly took a heavy toll on the already weary travelers. Some historical reports claim that Royce Oatman was seen crying by some of his family members, which goes to show you just how grueling this whole situation was.

It is also said that his family noted that Royce was desperate and disillusioned for much of the trip, having lost the faith that they could make it safely across the trail to California. They were surrounded by desolate wilderness— a vast desert behind them, and a massive mountain range up ahead, and they had to cross it all before they can safely make it to their destination.

The further they delved into the road, the more difficult things got. Lifting the carriages up hills and slopes was becoming grueling, not just the family members, but also the tired beasts. They also had to travel in scorching heat under the mercy of the relentless sun. Mrs. Oatman was the source of positivity during this grueling journey. She tended to her children's needs and did everything in her power to look after them while also supplying her husband with much-needed words of encouragement and moral support. The further they went, the less impact Mrs. Oatman's words seemed to have on her husband, who was put down by the gloomy road up ahead and the scarcity of resources around them.

This made the journey more intense for the children, who became alarmed and agitated when they noticed how overwhelmed, and gloomy their father was. They would always look to him for protection and depend on Royce Oatman for reassurance, but with everything that was happening and everything that awaited, Mr. Oatman was no longer the rock that they needed him to be. Royce tried to reassure his children and feign composure. He told his large family not to fear and that the Indians would not do them harm. It is said that Royce Oatman perceived the tensions between Indians and whites were often the whites' fault.

He would tell his children that if whites are generous and kind to Indians, then the natives would return the favor and act in kind. Unfortunately, this was not a correct assumption on Royce Oatman's side. As the events of that fateful day unfolded, he and most of his family members would be massacred in a terrible crime that would resonate across all ages and remain proof that kindness is not always met with kindness.

One can argue that Royce Oatman took an unnecessary risk by delving into the wilderness of the road with his family and with few supplies. One can even say that going on this campaign was foolish from the get-go and that those poor people were deceived by false prophets who promised them salvation in a promised land. All this, however, does not change the fact that innocent people were killed brutally, and they did not deserve to die.

CHAPTER THREE

～

The Oatman Massacre

Accounts differ as to when the horrible massacre took place. Some say it took place on February 18, 1851. Others claim it was March 18, not February. Regardless of the exact date, the outcome of the events of that fateful day remains the same: the horrible death of most of the Oatman's. It had been almost a year since the Oatman family first embarked on this perilous journey in search of a holy city, and their time together was about to come to an abrupt and tragic ending.

It is said that they were seven days or so into their trip in the wilderness when the tragedy happened—their progress was quite slow for the reasons we mentioned earlier, which ranged from the exhaustion of man and beast to the scarcity of the available resources. The Oatman family consisted of nine members by then: Royce Oatman and his wife along with their seven children, with another one soon to be born. Their ages ranged from one to seventeen, the oldest being Lucy Oatman.

On the fateful day of the massacre, a party of Plain Indians approached the Oatman family. The weather was relatively cool, and it was a bright morning. The family had been moving along the Gila River, which was later renamed the Oatman Flat. The party of Indians numbered 17 or 19, and they were armed with clubs, bows, and arrows. Royce Oatman greeted the Indian party friendlily, suppressing his fear and reminding himself of his theory: if the whites are kind to the Indians, then the Indians would have no reason to be hostile or hurt him or his family. Oatman greeted them in Spanish and welcomed them to sit down. The Indians wanted tobacco and pipes. Royce Oatman complied and gave them what they needed.

Together, they smoked as a gesture of goodwill and friendship. Getting greedy, the Indians then asked for something to eat because they were hungry. Royce Oatman knew that there were little supplies as it was, and his family needed every last bit of them, which he conveyed to the menacing party. He told them that they still had a very long journey ahead, and his family would starve if he gave them food. Eventually, though, he finally gave in and gave the Indians some bread and apologized for not having any more. This, however, was not enough to satisfy the Indian party.

They demanded more food, but Royce refused firmly and told them that he'd be starving his children if he gave them anything else. This was when things started escalating. One of the tribal members jumped into the Oatman wagon, demanding meat and shouting. He rummaged through their belongings, searching for any food they might have kept hidden. He asked for food again, but Royce refused. More Indians climbed into the wagon and started looting whatever goods they could find that would be of use. They tucked what they stole in their clothes, acting as if the Oatman's were not even there.

The Indians knew that the Oatman's were unarmed, so they stole whatever they wanted unchecked. Royce Oatman was smart enough not to provoke them, either. He watched them helplessly as they took what they needed, fearing any further aggression. Once they were done, the Indian party retreated shortly to confer amongst themselves. Royce proceeded to reload the wagon with their belongings, which had been haphazardly tossed outside. In her testimony later, Olive Oatman, who was almost 14 then, said that no members in the family provoked the Indians or showed any signs of aggression, which her brother Lorenzo also confirmed.

Conferring together, the Indians looked tensely down the road as if expecting an enemy to arrive or perhaps another party. Then, out of nowhere, they burst out shouting and attacked the Oatman family. Their clubs held high, and with terrifying battle cries, the Indians attacked the stunned family. Lorenzo Oatman, aged 14 or 15 at the time, was struck first. After the first club to the head, the boy crumpled to the ground in a pool of his own blood. He tried getting up, but another blow knocked him to the ground, leaving him to fight for his life. Royce tried to put up a fight, according to the survivors' tale, but he was overwhelmed by several of the Indians and quickly fell to the ground, also drenched in blood. Oatman's wife held on to her youngest and tried to save her, screaming and pleading for anyone to come to help them. Alas, the Oatman's were alone.

The poor woman was soon clubbed to death along with her youngest. The Oatman children Lucy, Charity Ann, Royce Jr., and Roland were all also clubbed mercilessly. Olive recollects seeing her family drenched in a gruesome puddle of blood, dead or dying. Only Olive and her younger sister Mary Ann (7 or 8 years old) were spared. They were held captives and dragged aside in the grip of two Indians. They watched in horror as the war party started looting the helpless Oatmans, who were either dead or moaning in pain, covered in blood. The Indians stripped the wagon down to its wheels and looted everything in it. They then unyoked the cows and oxen.

Lorenzo Oatman was unconscious and bleeding, and he was left for dead. He, too, managed to survive after the Indians left him, thinking he was either dead or dying. Lorenzo recalls that he soon regained consciousness to the terrible shrieks and cries of the Indians, along with the groans of his dying family. The Indians saw him move, and they emptied his pockets before throwing him off a cliff. *"Upon a careful examination of the spot, I estimated that he must have fallen twenty feet before he struck the rocky slope of the mesa. That he was not instantly killed or maimed beyond recovery seems miraculous. Strange discordant sounds, he tells us, grated upon his ears, gradually dying away, and then he heard "strains of such sweet music that completely ravished his senses,"* says J. Ross Browne in his book Adventures in the Apache Country where he examined the area.

And thus, the massacre of the Oatman family leaves a terrible trail of carnage that would be remembered to this very day. They were moments of great violence, but they were also moments of horror and fear that plagued the lonely family in the face of such cruelty and destruction. History tells us that this was not the only massacre committed by the Indians during those troubling few centuries. As we will explore in this upcoming segment, the Indians could be dangerous, and they were able to demonstrate terrible cruelty on occasions.

The Oatman family massacre of 1851 was not the only one committed by the Indians in the face of the white settlers. On such incident was the Indian Massacre of 1622.

The Colony of Virginia was the first truly enduring English Colony in North America by 1607. By 1622, the Indians were realized that the Europeans were there to stay with every intention of expanding, regardless of what this would do to the natives' land. This created hostility and anger within the natives, which culminated in the ruthless attack of 1622 that left hundreds dead. The attack was led by the Powhatan Confederacy leader Opchanacanough and his brother Opitchapam.

There were tensions in the early 1600s between the white settlers and the Powhatan Confederacy when the native Indians were starting to understand just how ambitious the settlers were. This eventually led to the first Powhatan war in 1609-1610, which was brutal and left many dead on both sides. This war eventually ended, however, and there was peace established by 1614, and the natives and settlers engaged in trade. The peace lasted for a while, and relations prospered between both sides. They were even friendly with one another and often visited each other's lands where they were welcomed. Natives would often visit the colonists and would-be guests in their homes, and vice versa. However, considering the expansion goals of the whites, this peace was not bound to last.

The initial settlement of the colonies was in Jamestown, but the settlers did not plan to stick to just that one establishment. Soon, they started spreading out from Jamestown and taking more land from the Powhatan Confederacy. In doing so, they were brutal and cruel to the natives and abused them. The settlers stole food and desecrated native ritual sites on purpose. They even destroyed the natives' crops in some locations. Naturally, for the Powhatan, this was not a situation to be accepted, and it could not last for long. The expansion of the white settlers was fueled by the tobacco trade, which helped them seize a lot of lands from the Powhatan in a short time.

This eventually led to the Powhatan fighting back, which resulted in the massacre of 1622. The attack was not spontaneous or accidental; it was carefully planned. The Powhatan wanted to send a message to the English settlers with this attack. For starters, they wanted to show just how powerful and formidable the Powhatan Confederacy was and that it was not an enemy to be taken lightly. If the English kept expanding and stealing land, they would be met with brute force. They also wanted to demoralize the colonizers and show them the kind of fate that awaited them if they kept the same course. Finally, the Powhatan hoped that this attack would scare the settlers enough so that they would return to their own country and leave these lands.

The first two goals were achieved with the massacre of 1622. The English were extremely demoralized, and they were also aware of the prowess of the Powhatan and that they were not an enemy to be taken lightly. They, however, had no plans of returning home and abandoning this fertile land with all its resources. The massacre eventually backfired and led to the English waging the second Powhatan war, which lasted from

1622 to 1626, which they won. The massacre proved disastrous for the Powhatan in the long run after the English won the second war. Trade was not allowed with certain tribes, and the settlers seized more lands. The tobacco trade boomed, and more land was taken for tobacco plantations. Come 1944, Opchanacanough launched another attack in 1944, which set off the third Powhatan war from 1644 to 1646, and this war ended with his captivity and consequent death.

The end of the third Powhatan war also marked the end of the Powhatan Confederacy. By 1646, a treaty dissolved the confederacy and established the reservation system for native Indians in the area. Moving past this slight historical background on the massacre, let's delve into the details and find out what really happened in 1622.

Jamestown was the first successful English settlement in North American, as we mentioned earlier, so it was no surprise that it would be the place of such a terrible massacre for the Indians to send a message to the English. Established in 1607, the Jamestown Colony of Virginia did not take much time to give birth to new conflict with the natives, in this case, the tribes of the Powhatan Confederacy. It probably came as no surprise to anyone that the whites' expansion would cause this much trouble. The natives of the Powhatan tribes had populated these lands for thousands of years. Their whole lives were connected to these parts, with rich cultural traditions and rituals deeply connected to the land.

It was 1492 when the Spanish arrived in the new world. They started with the West Indies upon arrival and then worked their way up to South and Central America over the years. They reached as far as Florida we know today as well as New York. They did not explore beyond Florida, but they did occasionally raid the coastal tribes and villages to kidnap natives to be sold into slavery. The history of that period is complex and filled with tragedies and terrible behavior on the explorers' side, which eventually led to worse horrors on the native Americans' side.

The English were a bit slower to expand into the New World, starting with a few settlements in the late 1500s in Virginia. Most of them did not survive and were not successful. Come 1607, the Indians knew who they were dealing with based on several experiences with the Europeans, none exactly nice. As for the Powhatan Confederacy, they did not resent the English when they first arrived because the settlers chose unusable lands to build their settlements. The Chief of the Powhatan, Chief Powhatan (also known as Wahunsenacah) then even thought that he might ally his people with the English against the Spanish and other hostile tribes in the country.

Chief Powhatan even ordered the supply of food and other supplies to the English, who were not prepared for this new world and often faced trouble adapting. Unfortunately, as is often the case, such kindness was treated with a sense of entitlement by the colonists, who came to expect such supplies and food instead of having to work for it. The good relations between the Powhatan and the colonists soon turned sour because the whites kept stealing food and land. They no longer tried to befriend the tribes and instead stole from them, testing the patience of the locals.

As time passed, the colonists kept stealing lands beyond Jamestown, as well as food. They treated the Powhatan as if they were subjects of the English King, more inferior subjects, though. When his goodwill gestures were treated with this entitlement and rewarded with theft of food and land, Chief Powhatan decided that things could not keep like this as the whites' true intentions were starting to show. *"Your coming is not for trade, but to invade my people and possess my country...Having seen the death of all my people thrice... I know the difference of peace and war better than any other country,"* said Chief Powhatan.

He ordered the colonist to stay within their settlements and told his men to kill any whites leaving the forts. These orders led to the period called the Starving Time of the Jamestown Colony, which is estimated to have led to the starvation and eventual death of two out of every three colonists due to this siege.

The Starving Time of 1609-1610 let the colonists know that their approach of open friendliness, and theft in the shadows, was not going to work anymore. By mid-1610, a new governor and several aristocrats arrived in Jamestown, and they had a different strategy from their predecessors. They did not care so much about friendly relations with the tribes. They were military men, and they thought of this problem as one that needed a military solution. The English decided not to compromise with the Powhatan, which started the first Powhatan war from 1610 to 1614. A guerilla war started with several raids and attacks from both sides that left many dead. The war was new to both sides, in its current form. The colonists were armed with muskets, while the natives had their bows and arrows and clubs. The Indians were naturally better guerilla warriors than the English, and they had better knowledge of the land. Their weapons were also more effective. The muskets took time to reload, while an arrow and bow took mere seconds.

While this gave an advantage to the Indians, the colonists had a bigger one: an infinite supply of men to throw at this war. Newcomers kept arriving at the new world to take the place of those who had fallen to the Indians. This numerical advantage was one that the Indian tribes naturally did not have. The English settlers also followed a ruthless strategy that kept gaining new ground. Whenever they conquered a village, they killed its people and fortified it. This kept the Indians on the back foot and continuously compromised the resources and lands that they used to wage this war. It also helped the English gain more ground and grew the area between Jamestown and the local villages.

The war lasted for a long time, and more settlers kept coming in with their weapons and cannons. They kept gaining new ground and expanding the settlements beyond Jamestown. Unfortunately for the Indians, one of those settlers who arrived into their country was John Rolfe, who came in 1610 with hybrid tobacco seeds that he wanted to experiment with. He planted the tobacco, and it turned out to be the most successful crop from the colonies. By the end of the war, he was very wealthy and had a massive plantation north of Jamestown. One Samuel Argall took over after Rolfe became ill in 1613, and it was him who kidnapped Chief Powhatan's daughter, Pocahontas, holding her for ransom.

To get his daughter back, Powhatan ransomed Pocahontas for the things that Argall wanted: weapons, tools, and prisoners. Argall kept the girl, though, as he claimed that the Chief did not honor the deal. Taking the name Rebecca after converting to Christianity, Pocahontas married John Rolfe in 1614, which ended the war and started an eight-year period of peace where trade prospered, and no lands were stolen. Pocahontas gave birth to Thomas Rolfe, and she died in 1617, while returning from England to Virginia. Chief Powhatan stepped down from the leadership of the confederacy, but he kept the peace for his grandson's sake. His half-brother eventually Opchanacanough became the Chief, known and respected among the tribal leaders of the Powhatan tribes.

Opchanacanough was not as interested in keeping the peace as his predecessor did, but he played along and kept the peace for a while. What drove

Opchanacanough's actions was something done by his predecessor. Wahunsenacah had sent some of his trusted circle with Pocahontas to England, including her brother-in-law Tomocomo. Wahunsenacah ordered him to observe the English and report back to him. Tomocomo's report on the English was that they were not to be trusted, which the next Chief Powhatan Opchanacanough took to heart, it seemed.

Opchanacanough kept the peace and even pretended to accept the English effort to preach Christianity, which was quite important for the settlers, who wanted more native Indians to follow in Pocahontas' trail and convert. The Chief encouraged his people to take an interest in conversion. He himself showed an interest in learning about Christianity, which naturally led the settlers to believe that peace was prospering. Those who controlled the colony truly believed that by 1621, things were better than they had ever been, as shown by their accounts. Peace prospered between the natives and the colonists until the massacre of 1622.

The first English government in the colony was the House of Burgesses, and it was established by 1619 to keep law and order. One of the things it claimed to have set as a priority was reviewing any wrongdoings committed against the Natives. In 1621, an incident took place that threatened the peace. Opchanacanough general, or war chief, Nemattanew, was killed by the whites when they accused him of killing a colonist to steal his clothes. The Powhatan Chief, however, did not react. He accepted the judgment and even agreed that his war chief was killed fairly. He let things go.

Around that same period, Opchanacanough and his brother invited the tribes for a ceremony that was allegedly in honor of his predecessor, who died around 1618. It is believed, however, that Opchanacanough set this meeting to prepare for the massacre and coordinate their efforts with the tribes. The colonists suspected nothing then since such a ceremony seemed reasonable. It is also believed that the Powhatan were gathering information heavily back then to learn all they could about the colonists and the settlements they'd be in and the best way possible to execute this attack.

March 22, 1622, was Good Friday, and things were as normal as they had ever been. The settlers went to work on their farms and opened their shops, life was calm, and no one expected any surprise attacks. Early in the morning, several Indians slithered into the settlements along the James River. They knocked on the doors of the white colonists and asked to be let in. The settlers did not suspect a thing; after all, many of those who knocked were familiar faces and had previously been welcomed into their homes. The Indians were also unarmed, which meant there was no cause for alarm. They were offered food and drink, and the Indians accepted them.

Then, chaos ensued.

The Indians suddenly grabbed anything they could find at their disposal. They used kitchen knives and stewpots. They reached for the whites' personal guns. Whatever they could find to use a weapon, they got it, and they used it to kill everyone in the house. This did not happen in one or two houses. The attack was well-coordinated, and it happened on a massive scale that was not random. It is said that the attack was so surprising and shocking, that many of the colonists died before they even grasped that they were being attacked. Families were slaughtered, and houses were burned with the bodies in them. Fortunately for Jamestown, they were given enough warning when the chaos ensued, so they had time to prepare their defenses.

It is said that the warning was given by a young Indian who lived in one of the colonists' houses. Whatever the case might be, Jamestown was warned, which probably saved many lives. However, it is estimated that about 347 people still died on the day of the massacre. Some estimates put the dead at 400, but it is impossible to find out exactly how many died. They were hundreds, with many more wounded. There was a children's college in Henricus Colony, which was completely destroyed, as was the hospital. It is also said that the Powhatan took 20 women captives after the widespread attacks until some were ransomed; others lived with the Powhatan until they died.

In the wake of the attack, the English were shocked. With settlements still aflame across the area, the English found themselves stunned by the wide-scale and the brutality of the attack. Small skirmishes and raids were not entirely uncommon, but nothing of this scale was heard of. The Powhatan could have killed many more. It was only Jamestown that was fortified, and there were still many colonists spread out in the region, panicked and defenseless. Attacking then would have left far more casualties and no survivors. Opchanacanough, however, did not see the point. The attack was successful, and the message was delivered. He instead withdrew his warriors and did nothing. He believed that the white colonists would act as an Indian tribe would when defeated: flee.

Opchanacanough thought that the colonists would quickly pack their things and leave their lands for good. Needless to say, his judgment was far from accurate. He misjudged the settlers and those backing them in England, who had no intentions of retreating. Many more people died in the aftermath of the massacre, which led to the destruction of many of the whites' crops. The colonists quickly had to resort to peace again and started to trade once more just so they would not starve. The rest, as they say, is history. Another Powhatan war soon broke out, and the colonists took advantage of the massacre to seize more native lands and displace their people. Many more people would die over the next few decades, and more would be displaced.

The massacre of 1622 would live in infamy until this very day. It went to show that the Indians could be as equally brutal and ruthless as the colonists. While some might say that their actions were a foolish attempt to scare the settlers away, the fact of the matter remains that they slaughtered unarmed colonists and killed entire families that opened their doors to welcome them to their homes. The massacre of 1622 was not random or an act of ungratefulness by the Indians. It was carefully planned and executed as a response to years of abuse by the colonists toward the Indians, which the whites were not shy about labeling them 'barely human.' Whether or not such a violent response was warranted is up for the reader to decide. In any case, the horrors of colonization continued on for many more years, with more violent crimes on either side.

The Oatman girls were not the first settlers to be captured by the Indians throughout the years. In the Peach Tree War, many were taken, and others were killed by the Indians. New Sweden was a Swedish colony along the Delaware River in America, lasting from 1638 to 1655. This colony was created at a time when Sweden was established as one of the greater military powers in the world, and they too wanted a piece of the new lands of America. The colony of New Sweden was a close ally of the Susquehannock tribes, and for years, relationships prospered between the two, and there was active trade. The Swedish had purchased the land from the Susquehannock when they arrived, so it was a fair trade, and therefore, there was no tensions between the allies.

The area was previously partially occupied by the Dutch and the English, but they could never really get their foot in and did not have a stronghold over the land. The Susquehannocks also did not trust the Dutch due to their association with other settlers whom the Susquehannock considered enemies. The English and the Dutch did not like having a new player and did not take kindly to Sweden's claim to the land. Meanwhile, the colony of New Sweden had excellent relations with the Indians, who supplied them with fur and pelts. The Indians even supplied the Swedes with customers to buy all those European goods. In return, New Sweden became a safe haven for the Susquehannocks where they could live in mutual peace and engage in friendly relations with the Swedes.

The English and the Dutch quickly refused to acknowledge Sweden's claim to the colony, and tensions quickly arose. The Dutch especially were concerned that Sweden's growing influence would threaten theirs. So, they tried to gather more forces to consolidate their power by combining the members of several forces along the disputed area. New Sweden's governor, Johan Printz, did not accept such provocation and decided to expel the Dutch. He attacked Fort Casimir in 1654, which was where the Dutch forces relocated to consolidate their numbers. Printz managed to expel the Dutch, and thus the new colony was completely under the control of New Sweden.

The Dutch retaliated, and they mounted an attack to reclaim control over the colonies and forts of New Sweden. This caused tensions to rise with the Susquehannock, who were not ready to lose their trading relations and peace with the Swedes. It is also believed that a certain incident sparked the attack that we will outline in a moment. New Netherland colonists talked of a murder of a young native Indian girl. They said a Dutch settler killed her, allegedly, for stealing a peach, which gave name to the events that were soon to transpire. This caused further tensions with the local tribes.

The Susquehannock Indians had consolidated power earlier when they took control over the Lenape Indians. This allowed them to amass a significant force of 600 warriors that were gathered from multiple tribes. They launched their attack on September 15, 1655. The 600 warriors descended on the narrow streets of New Amsterdam, Lower Manhattan now, and destroyed everything in sight. The attack was a surprise, and the colony was undefended since most of the garrison was still in New Sweden. The Indians did not stop at New Amsterdam; they later moved across the Hudson River and attacked Pavonia (Hoboken and Jersey City today).

Estimates vary on how many were killed in the Susquehannocks' attack. It is estimated that over 20 Dutch settlers were killed. Dozens of settlers were held hostages in the attack. The Susquehannocks attacked farms in Staten Island, Harlem, and the Bronx, too. When the Dutch eventually returned, they found their crops burned, and many of their horses either killed or set free. Things were chaotic. Fortunately, the captives were ransomed in exchange for blankets, ammunition, and wampum.

In the aftermath of the attack, a few years later, the Dutch eventually repurchased the rights to the lands of the Susquehannock. This incident goes to show how quickly things were likely to escalate back then and that greed was mostly what motivated the colonists. In their fight amongst each other to lay claim to as many lands as possible, it was often the Indians that were harmed and their lands and homes either stolen or destroyed. The Indians, however, often retaliated in kind, if not worse. Their attacks were brutal and surprising, and they often left entire colonies burning with many dead, and they often took captives to be ransomed—not all would make it through until they were ransomed, though.

The Nine Men's Misery is one of the worst incidents that ever took place during the Indian Wars, and it lives in infamy to this very day. This massacre showed just how brutal and bloodthirsty the Indians could be if pushed, and this terrible crime was one that shook the world back then.

King Philip's War started in 1675, and it lasted three years between the Indians of New England and the colonists (and some of their Indian allies as well). The war is considered by many to be among the worst war between Indians and settlers. In 1676, during the height of the war, a fierce battle ensued between Narragansetts Indians and Plymouth Colony troops led by Captain Michael Pierce.

Pierce set to pursue Narragansetts Indians who had wreaked havoc in several colonies, including Rhode Island towns and Plymouth. Sadly for Pierce and his company of 60 colonists and 20 Wampanoag Indians, they caught up with the Narragansetts. It turns out an ambush awaited them, and the colonists and their native allies fell right into it. The forces led by Pierce fought the Narragansetts for hours, but it was futile. They were vastly outnumbered, and there was no way that they could win this battle. It was near Rhode Island where they were ambushed, and the colonist forces suffered one of their greatest defeats during this war. Nearly all were wiped out, including Captain Pierce, while their enemies only lost a few Narragansetts tribesmen.

Nine of the colonists survived the onslaught, and they were taken as prisoners by the Indians. The prisoners were taken to a location in Cumberland, Rhode Island, where nine of them were brutally tortured to death by the Narragansetts. The bodies were found and buried by English soldiers who found them and piled some stones over the burial site to make a memorial for those fallen in this attack. To this day, despite the site's desecration several times, the memorial lives on, and there is a pile of rocks on the site now that anyone can see to look back on the memory of much more uncivilized times.

There are always contradicting tales about this time in history. It is more than likely that there are more sides to this story than the one we had. Did the Narragansetts really torture nine prisoners to death? It is possible. Was this a made-up story created to further fuel the hate toward the 'savage Indians'? That is also possible, considering the prevailing narrative among colonists about how brutal and merciless the Indians were and how they were not much different from wild beasts. The one thing we know is that there is a burial site and a memorial to this very day in Cumberland, and in it, several men were buried.

The Pueblo Revolt is another famous incident that took place in 1680. Also known as Pope's Rebellion, this is the incident where the Pueblo native Indians rose against the Spanish colonizers and slaughtered hundreds of them in Santa Fe de Nuevo México, which is a bigger area than what we know today as New Mexico. By the end of this uprising, over 400 Spaniards had been killed, and thousands of others were driven out of the settlement.

The Pueblo native Indians did not have it as peacefully as some other natives across the continent. While some tribes in certain areas had known years of peace and trade with the colonists, the Pueblo Indians were subjected to one wave after the other of soldiers and missionaries, and settlers. These incursions were rarely peaceful, and they were often violent, and there would often be clashes between the colonists and the local Indians. In 1598, one Spanish colonist called Juan de Oñate led a group of soldiers (and priests, servants, and women and children even) in a campaign that changed the region forever. They slaughtered thousands of the Pueblo Indians and enslaved others. The brutal campaign did not stop there. All men aged 25 or older had their feet cut off in one of the most infamous massacres of that era.

Fear of the Spaniards spread among the natives for many years after the massacres committed by the colonists. Tensions arose in the 1670s when a drought hit the region, causing famine and disease that affected the natives and made them vulnerable to attacks by rival tribes such as the Apache. In 1675, things escalated when the governor executed 3 Pueblo healers after accusing them of practicing sorcery, and a fourth captive killed himself. Many other healers were arrested and publicly flogged, and they were also imprisoned. In a fit of rage, the Pueblo Indians attacked Santa Fe and demanded the release of the prisoners, which the governor had to concede to since many of his men were away fighting the Apache. One of those released prisoners was an Indian called Popé.

After his release, Popé and other tribal leaders from the Pueblo Indians planned the revolt to end the horrible enslavement of their people. It took five years for Popé to gather support from several Pueblo towns and villages, and many did, in fact, join his cause—though some opted out of the confrontation. Preparing for the battle, the Pueblo Indians prepared with their primitive bows and arrows, and it is said that some Apache and Navajo Indians might have joined their ranks for the revolt. Popé promised the rebels that the gods would reward them with peace and health once they killed the colonists and expelled them from their land.

The plan set forth by Popé was simple: The Pueblo Indians living in every town would kill the Spanish colonists in their area, and then they would join forces to march on Santa Fe to kill or expel any remaining Spaniards who would put up a fight. The plan was to commence on August 11 of 1680, and messengers were dispatched across the region with the time to start the uprising. On August 9, though, some Indian leaders warned the Spanish colonists of the revolt, and two young Indians were captured with the coded message. They were tortured to reveal the meaning of the messages they carried. Popé had originally ordered the uprising to commence on August 10, not 11, but the message did not reach all the Pueblo Indians on time, so some rose on the 11th according to plan.

And thus, the Pueblo revolt began. The Indians stole the colonists' horses and blocked all roads leading to Santa Fe to stop them from running. Doing so, they began attacking the Spanish settlements and looting them. It is estimated that 400 colonists were killed, including women and children as well as some missionaries. The attack was brutal and killed anyone in sight, even priests. Some survivors managed to flee to Santa Fe, but by August 13, all Spanish settlements in New Mexico were decimated, with many dead. Then, the rebels moved to lay siege to Santa Fe and cut off the water supply to the city.

Things were dire for the Spanish colonists, so the governor of New Mexico gathered all his remaining forces and barricaded himself in the Palace of Governors, and they fought the Pueblo Indians and forced them to retreat, suffering heavy losses in the process. The Spaniards then fled the city and retreated south. The Puebloans kept a close eye on the colonists, but they did not attack them, not even when they were transporting Indian slaves out of the area by train.

This did not mark the end of the aggression between the Pueblo Indians and the Spaniards. The colonists attempted to reclaim New Mexico the following year, and they mounted another attack.

The Lachine Massacre is yet another example of violence between Indians and Settlers. New France was the colony that the French made for themselves in North America. Peace reigned for 20 years in that area, but after two decades, the French and the English declared war on one another; the peace was about to end. It was earlier agreed upon by a treaty that any tensions between the European colonists would not spread to affect the colonial territories or the indigenous people. When the French and English went into war, this was not the case. It was a proxy war of sorts, with either party prompting their indigenous allies to wage attacks on the enemy.

The Iroquois Indians, who committed this massacre, had tense relations with the French for years. The French were vicious in their attack on the traditional lifestyle of the natives, which drove many of the local tribes out of their homes in fear of being hurt, or worse, dying in the constant raids and attacks. The cultural invasion of the French was one of the prime factors that led to the Lachine massacre eventually, as the Indians resented the French for their constant intrusion on their culture and traditions. While peace was often negotiated between the Iroquois Indians and the French, it was always fickle.

There was also an economic angle to the mutual resentment. The Iroquois wanted a bigger part of the fur trade, which the French monopolized. When the war between the English and the French erupted, tensions came to a head. The British in New York prompted the Iroquois to attack any New France settlements they can find in an attempt to destroy French morale and strike a blow to their expansion efforts. The French settlements were also poorly if even, defended. There were many remote villages and towns that could not be properly fortified, and there weren't even enough men to defend them.

The Lachine massacre took place on August 5, 1689. About 1,500 Iroquois warriors used the cover of night to sneak into the unprotected settlement of Lachine. They traveled by boat and covered the distance stealthily. The colonists were asleep at the time of the attack, unsuspecting of the horrors they were about to be subjected to. The Indian warriors enclosed the colonist homes, waiting for the signal to attack. The brutal attack began, and the massacre was ruthless. The Iroquois broke into the homes and dragged the settlers into the streets, slaying many. Some colonists tried to fortify themselves within buildings, but those buildings were set on fire with them inside. Then, all the Iroquois had to do was wait for the settlers to flee the flaming buildings, and they killed them one by one.

Estimates vary on how many fell in the horrible massacre. Some sources say it was 24 French settlers; others put the number as high as 250. About 70 prisoners were taken alive, too. In any case, a lot of people died that night, and many were taken captive. François Vachon de Belmont was the superior of the Sulpicians of Montreal (a society of apostolic life) had written this on the horrible incident:

"*After this total victory, the unhappy band of prisoners was subjected to all the rage which the cruelest vengeance could inspire in these savages. They were taken to the far side of Lake St. Louis by the victorious army, which shouted ninety times while crossing to indicate the number of prisoners or scalps they had taken, saying, we have been tricked, Ononthio, we will trick you as well. Once they had landed, they lit fires, planted stakes in the ground, burned five Frenchmen, roasted six children, and grilled some others on the coals and ate them.*"

While some prisoners were ransomed, and others escaped, it is estimated that over forty were never seen or heard from again after the Lachine massacre. Some say they were adopted into the Iroquois, including young girls not much older than Olive Oatman. Others were most likely killed. Some of the survivors claimed that some prisoners were tortured, burned, and then eaten, as demonstrated by the above quote. Some of the survivors also bore torture marks and spoke of the horrors they were subjected to at the hands of the Iroquois.

We will never know if such accounts of cannibalism are true or exaggerated by the survivors to amplify the savagery and brutality of the native Indians. Accounts of what really happened are missing from the natives' history, so we have only the French sources to go back to. Still, torture of the enemy prisoners was not uncommon by native Indians, and it was even viewed as a way to honor enemy soldiers. It was indeed a common practice among many indigenous tribes.

In these previous pages, we have taken a closer look into some of the massacres and atrocities committed by native Indians to the colonists and their allies. It was an attempt to show the other side of the coin and a different perspective into the brutal history of these few centuries in the history of America. It also goes to show that the Indians could be brutal and ruthless, as shown by the incidents above and the murder of the Oatman family. The Oatman's were not the first family to be slaughtered by the Indians, and they were not also the last. Many had fallen in this gruesome period of history, many of whom were children and women.

It can be debated that colonists' soldiers and men knew what they were doing and what they were getting into by traveling to a foreign land and stealing the resources and lands of the indigenous people. The atrocities of the colonizers are too many to list and have spanned centuries, almost bordering on the genocide of the native peoples of North America. However, did such atrocities warrant the slaughter of women and children by the Indians? Were the infants and little children guilty of their parents' sins and attempts to colonize other people's lands? These are questions that cannot be answered so simply.

Unfortunately for the Oatman's, a history of blood and violence permeated the lands, and there was much bad blood between the Indians and the white settlers. The road they took was dangerous, and the Indians on it could be ruthless, and the Oatman's paid a heavy price for such a risky venture.

CHAPTER FOUR

❧

Captive in a Strange World

Our story picks up after Olive and Mary Ann Oatman fall into the captivity of the Plain Indians. The sisters were extremely shaken by the gruesome deaths of their family, and they had no idea what fate awaited them. They were both children at that time, and the future did not look bright for the Oatman sisters. They were taken captives by the Indians, and there was no telling what would happen then.

The sisters recount what happened to them after their family was massacred. The Indians split into two groups: the first handled the looted belongings of the Oatman family, carrying them to their destination, and they led the animals as well. The other group kept an eye on the captive sisters, shepherding them to a campsite that was about half a mile away. The Indians rested and had some food, even offering Olive and Mary Ann some. The girls refused to take any food from the men who had just slaughtered their entire family. The Indians then continued their journey, but not before taking both girls' shoes off. This was done to stop Olive and Mary Ann from escaping, as their feet would not be able to handle all the rocks and pebbles that the area was littered with, not to mention cactus, which would have destroyed their feet.

In this grueling and terrible journey, the young Mary Ann was unable to carry on for much longer, weakened by exhaustion and the turmoil of this terrible ordeal. She had to be carried on the back of one of the Indians. When the sisters would ask for water or to rest for a while, they would be poked with lances. The indigenous natives marched for a few days, heading to their home village. The sisters recall that all the remaining Oatman animals were slaughtered, oxen and cows. According to Olive Oatman, it was three or four days later when the convoy arrived at their native village. For the Oatman sisters, this was not where their suffering ended, but rather, began.

Olive recounted a life of abuse and mistreatment at the hands of their captors. They were forced into labor as they lived with the tribe, even in their poor health. The sisters were expected to bring firewood, tend to fires, and perform a myriad of tasks such as gathering glass seeds. At first, as was the custom among native Indians, the sisters were treated harshly as captives of the enemy, which was not unusual. They were treated in a way such that Olive later said that she thought they would kill her and her sister.

The sisters were smart, however. Over the course of a year or so since their capture, they learned how to avoid the wrath of the Indians and avoid being beaten up. They slowly integrated themselves into the tribal lifestyle and assimilated into this new life that they were forced into. Olive even learned the language of those who killed her family and captured her and her sister, presumably Tolkepaya. It is believed that the captors of the sisters were Western Yavapais.

Later in time, roughly a year or so after their capture by the Yavapai, another tribe came to visit, the Mohave, presumably. The Mohave had friendly relations with the Yavapai, and such trade visits were not uncommon. The Mohave learned about the captured sisters and wanted to trade for them. Things were about to improve for the captured girls. The leader of the Mohave was a young woman, and according to Olive, she was the daughter of the tribe's chief, and she was "beautiful, intelligent, well-spoken, fluent in the languages of both tribes." Moreover, the tribal woman felt for the captured girls and wanted to help them, and sympathized with these rough conditions they found themselves in.

The young girls were asked if they would prefer to travel with the Mohave or stay with the Yavapais. Olive and Mary Ann were smart enough not to answer such a murky question, fearing that it could mean more beatings and ill-treatment if they were sentenced to stay with their original captors. The next few hours were difficult ones for the sisters as their fate was being decided among tribal elders, each presenting different arguments as to the fate of the girls. Eventually, fortunately for the Oatman sisters, it was decided that they would be sold to the Mohave, or at the very least, traded for horses, blankets, and other supplies that the tribe needed.

Thus, Olive and Mary Ann left their initial captivity and traveled with the Mohaves for roughly 10 days through the desert, another arduous journey to get to their new home. It is presumed that they were taken to an area near the Colorado River where California, Nevada, and Arizona intersect. This was not the Bashan that the Oatman family patron had intended to take his family to, but it was certainly better than their earlier life of being beating and forced labor.

At first, the Oatman sisters were taken to the tribe chief's home, where they were told of how their life would be in the upcoming years. They were expected to work for their lodgings. The Oatman sisters were to work the fields, picking berries and harvesting wheat and corn, while also collecting wood and doing other tasks. Things were not as bad as with the Yavapai, though. According to the sisters, the Mohaves had better shelters than the Yavapai, and they were also much kinder to Olive and Mary Ann. They were even given grounds to grow wheat, corn, and melons.

As time passed in this new life, Olive and Marry Ann began forging true friendships and friendly relationships with the Mohave people. Many were kind to them, and they were not treated with the harshness of the Yavapai. It is even said that the chief's wife was very kind to them and treated them like daughters— she was the one who gave them the lands to sow and harvest. The sisters were also friends with the chief's daughter, who was nice to them. Olive later expressed her deep affection for those two women, even after her captivity had ended.

Olive was later given the Mohave name Spantsa, which translates in their language into unquenchable thirst or lust. In another step that showed how integrated they were into the Mohave tribal life, the sisters were tattooed. It was a very common tradition among the Mohave people and a way for the Mohave to be identified in the afterlife. With these unique tattoos, when a Mohave enters the lands of the dead, they would be recognized by their ancestors and members of the tribe. *"They pricked the skin in small regular rows on our chins with a very sharp stick until they bled freely,"* Olive wrote later. She and her sister received these tribal tattoos on the chin as well as single lines on each arm. The tattoos were made with pigments of the juice of weeds mixed with ground blue powder from river rocks. This mixture is then rubbed into the bleeding lines.

Reverend Royal B. Stratton was the person who sponsored and oversaw the publication of Olive's captivity story, not long after she returned to the whites, and it is often said that he took much liberty in describing the sister's time with the Mohave. According to that tale, Olive and her sister had been forced to bear those tattoos to be marked as slaves, but this is not entirely accurate because it was not a Mohave tradition, as we explained above. The Mohave only cared about their people being recognized in the afterlife, so they did not really care about tattooing slaves. Some also claimed that the lines on Olive's face were even and clear, which show's that she was not tattooed against her will.

In 1853, a terrible drought descended on the entire region, and it killed many people. Crops dried up, and many Indians starved. Sadly, Mary Ann was one of those who died in those drought years. She grew weaker from lack of proper nutrition until she was unable to accompany her sister in the hunt for seeds and grains. Olive estimated that it was around 1855 or 1856 when her young sister died. Olive buried Mary Ann, who had died along with many other Mohave in those difficult years. Another indicator that Olive had commanded respect within the Mohave is how she was allowed to say farewell to Mary Ann. The Mohave's tradition was to cremate their dead, but Olive was allowed to bury Mary Ann.

One of the most heavily contended questions concerning the Oatman sisters is whether or not they were happy during their time with the Mohave. Some claimed that Olive was held against her will, and she was a prisoner and an unhappy one. Others say that she had completely assimilated into this new life and had found some happiness with the Indians. Olive Oatman's story itself sometimes is contradictory, or at least the statement attributed to her are.

In the book published by Reverend Royal B. Stratton, Olive is said to have been unhappy and kept against her will, according to her own story allegedly. Yet, a Mohave tribesman (and basically the Mohave's unofficial historian) called Llewelyn Barrackman once said in an interview that it is most likely that Olive was adopted into the tribe and treated as one of the locals since she was given a Mohave name, which was something that only happened to those who have fully integrated themselves into the tribe. Evidence that supports the claim that Olive was happy was the fact that she did not try to escape and did not attempt to ask for help when a group of white travelers visited the Mohave while she was with them! The white visitors were supposedly railroad surveyors, and they spent a week with the Mohave in the spring of 1854. Olive could have revealed herself and asked to be rescued, but she did not. Reports claim that Mary Ann was alive, too, in that year, and she too did not reveal herself to the whites, which were estimated to be about 200 individuals.

It is even reported that years after all this, Olive Oatman traveled to New York to meet a Mohave leader called Irataba, and she spoke with him about 'old-time,' which might imply that she thought fondly about her time with the Mohaves. An anthropologist called A. L. Kroeber wrote the following in an article he published about the Oatman girls' captivity: *"The Mohaves always told her she could go to the white settlements when she pleased, but they dared not go with her, fearing they might be punished for having kept a white woman so long among them, nor did they dare to let it be known that she was among them."* Did the Mohaves really tell Olive she could leave whenever she pleases? This might be a question to which we will never get an answer. Olive said in an interview that the Mohaves told her to go but feared accompanying her, as Kroeber had mentioned, but she argued that she could not leave on her own because she did not know the way.

In 1860, however, Olive noted in her lectures that her young sister often yearned to join her parents in the 'better world' they had gone to. Despite Mary Ann's apparent unhappiness, she died of starvation that affected everyone equally back then, so there is no evidence to support that the Mohaves were particularly negligent with the whites in their village. Some even claimed that Olive, too, would have died if the chief's wife, Aespaneo, had not made her some gruel to keep her alive. Olive said that Aespaneo fed her in secret while much of the village people went hungry, which could explain why Olive was eternally grateful and spoke fondly of the tribal woman and her daughter, who treated her like family. Later in her life, Olive would most often speak fondly of the Mohave and how they were much kinder to her than her earlier captors.

One of the contributing to Olive's desire to stay with the Mohave's, especially after her sister's death, may have been the fact that she thought that she was alone in the world. As far as Olive knew, her entire family was slaughtered in the attack. She had no idea that Lorenzo survived and believed that she had no immediate family remaining. The Mohave, however, treated her as one of their own and welcomed her into their tribe.

Some rumors and tales spoke of Olive marrying one of the Mohave and bearing two children, but there is little proof that something like that happened, and most historians agree that this is false. Llewelyn Barrackman said that if Olive had married a Mohave and bore his children, "we would all know." He made another point that Olive's children would have stood out considering their mixed race, and they could have been easily traced back to Olive. It is also argued that Olive could not bear children, considering that she married after returning to the white community and never bore children still. The anthropologist A. L. Kroeber interviewed one particular Mohave called Musk Melon, fifty years after Olive was ransomed to the whites, and Melon is said to have known Olive well. Melon said that he knew nothing about Olive ever getting married to one of his people.

The truth about the Oatman girls' captivity will always be vague, and the tales about what happened to them still contradict to this very day. As we mentioned earlier, much of that controversy can be attributed to Royal Stratton. He interviewed Olive around 1857 or 1858 and wrote his bestselling book about her capture, first titled Life Among the Indians and later renamed to Captivity of the Oatman Girls, where he documented the five years in total that Olive had spent with the Indians. Later, Olive gave lectures about what happened to her with the Indians, and there were often many discrepancies compared to the book and many of the details varied on several occasions.

In Stratton's book and her lectures, one detail that Olive remained consistent about was the fact that the Indians never "*offered the least unchaste abuse to me,*" whether the Mohaves or the Yavapais. Olive denied any allegations of rape or sexual intercourse with tribesmen. Yet, Susan Thompson, who was her best childhood friend and later reunited with her, stated that Olive married a Mohave man and bore him two boys, which caused her depression upon returning to the white community. Olive denied these claims.

As for Olive's lectures of her own accounts, they contained several inaccuracies, starting with the identity of her captors, whom she identified as Apache. Most historians, however, believe they were Yavapais. In her lectures, she also claimed that she and her sister were tattooed so they could be identified if they escaped, and it was a mark of slavery. This, however, contradicts the Mohave tradition, that we talked about earlier, of only tattooing their people to be recognized in the afterlife.

It is not unlikely that Olive had mixed feelings about the Mohave. Maybe she resented living with people other than hers, especially after the horrible massacre of her family at the hands of indigenous people. She could have felt that way and still come to love the Mohave and enjoy her time with them. Humans are complex beings and are capable of feeling complex, often contradicting sentiments. It is possible that, after her ransom, Olive was driven into anti-native fervor, especially by the Reverend Stratton, whose book about her ordeal was filled with such rhetoric and carried hateful sentiments against the Indians, often describing them as savages and such. Olive, too, started using that label and described them as savages in her lectures.

However, upon her return, there were stories and reports about how Olive was unhappy and depressed. Her actions (in private at least) did not go with her describing the Indians as savages as a whole. It was the Mohave that saved her from her captors that murdered her family. The Mohave gave her and her sister a home and land to sow and harvest as their own. They treated them with kindness, though they often teased her, as shown by the name given to Olive, which loosely translates to unquenchable lust, as we mentioned earlier. All in all, they were not hostile toward her, and she often spoke of them fondly in smaller settings, despite calling them savages frequently in her lectures and making the above-mentioned claims about her tattoo.

We will never truly know the exact details of what happened to Olive and Mary Ann in captivity. We will also never know Olive's exact feelings toward the Indians because she might have had great affection for them but was forced to hide it. Relations between colonists and Indians were often tense, and such mingling was to be frowned upon. Had she changed her story from one of a captive girl forced to stay with the Mohave into one where she grew to love the people and the place and nature, Olive might have led a much more difficult life, even among the whites. It did not help that she bore a tattoo as a constant reminder of her past, which we'll also explore in a bit. But the pressure of aligning herself with the prevailing narrative that the Indians were savage monsters was most likely too big for anyone to handle, regardless of how Olive truly felt about them.

CHAPTER FIVE

~

Finding Freedom

As you recall, Lorenzo, Olive's brother, was thrown off a cliff (or he might have tumbled in some retellings) and was either left for dead by the Indians, believed to be dead, or they might have missed him altogether. Whatever it was, fate deemed it that the young Lorenzo would survive the horrible attack. The young boy naturally did not feel fortunate or blessed to have survived the massacre. He climbed up the hill and saw the horrible sight of his family, mutilated and left in pools of their own blood. Despite the horrendous sight, however, Lorenzo was alerted to one thing: two of his sisters went missing. He knew they were probably captured by the marauding Indian party, and for the years to come, Lorenzo never forgot about them.

Weary from the blood loss caused by his injuries, and the haunting sight of his murdered family, Lorenzo left the scene in search of help. He crawled and dragged himself to the nearby river, straining to remain conscious. He reached the river and quenched the thirst that he thought would kill him. After drinking from the river, worn out by his injuries, young Lorenzo slept for a while, hoping that this would all be a horrible dream from which he would wake up to find his family alive and well. Alas, a dream it was not.

Lorenzo awoke to find that he was all alone, with congealed blood on his head and bruises all over his body. Adamant not to surrender to his fate, Lorenzo decided to make his way back to the Pimo villages that his family rested in, a lifetime ago, it seemed. The villages were roughly a hundred miles away, and it was a near-impossible journey for a young, injured man with no food or water. The Pimo villages, however, were the nearest safe place he knew of, and thus, Lorenzo set out on his journey. For two days, he tried covering as much distance as he could. He sometimes walked, and others crawled on his hands and knees. He would stop whenever fate graced him with a bush whose shade could shield him from the scorching sun and its heat.

Lorenzo was burdened by exhaustion that led to delirium and, worst of all, the image of his slaughtered family. He was also weighed down by the fear that Indians might cross his path again and finish what they started. It did not take long for Lorenzo to be overwhelmed by the pain and exhaustion, and he kept growing weaker with the lack of food and water. He eventually let his body drop to the ground and awaited his death. It is said that Lorenzo awoke from this delirious sleep by the sound of nearby wolves who found a helpless prey and were intent on feasting on it. He fought them off by throwing rocks and occasionally striking the ones that were close.

On the next afternoon, Lorenzo was dragging his feet across a canyon with no cover or shelter. He came across two Pimo Indians riding on horses. The Indians were surprised to see someone in this desolate wilderness and nocked their arrows in preparation to strike down this wraith that appeared out of nowhere. Lorenzo spoke to them in Spanish and told them that he was an American, begging them to spare his life. The Indians lowered their weapons and approached him, sympathetic. He told them what had happened to him and his family, and they expressed sympathy for his plight. The Indians offered him some bread and water, which young Lorenzo accepted with great enthusiasm.

The two Indians told Lorenzo to wait in his place for their return, but the boy naturally was distrustful of all natives. He thus commenced walking again, praying that he would be saved. If there is such a thing as a miracle, the sequence of events that followed might be labeled as such. Walking aimlessly across the desert, Lorenzo spotted two wagons approaching from afar. As they approached, the boy was overtaken by a wave of excitement and powerful emotions. These were white wagons, and Lorenzo knew they had to be American. Overwhelmed by emotions and his pains, Lorenzo fell unconscious. He awakened an hour or so later by a familiar voice calling him by name and asking him what had happened. It was Wilder—a member of one of the two families from the wagon train that opted to stay behind while Royce Oatman, his father, moved forward. The families of Wilder and Kelly had rested and decided to try and make it to Fort Yuma.

Lorenzo came to it again and found himself back and safe among the Pimos. A few days later, after regaining some of his strength, Lorenzo returned with some men to bury his dead family. *"We buried the bodies of the father, mother, and babe in one common grave,"* he said in a later recollection of the events. There was no way of burying the dead family in the ground due to the volcanic rock soil. So, they gathered the bodies together and covered them in a cairn. Some say the bodies were reburied several times over the next few years.

With his family buried, Lorenzo made it to an emigrant encampment where he never lost the hope of finding his sisters. Many would have given up hope that their siblings were alive after such a horrible massacre, but that was never an option for Lorenzo, who kept an eye out for any information for the next few years. Lorenzo tried to make a living over the coming years, all while trying to discover any new information about his kidnapped sisters. Taking up primary residence in Fort Yuma, Lorenzo tried in vain to get the military authorities to help him look for his sisters, but it was pointless. They had no interest in sending search parties for two girls who might be dead for all they knew.

However, one Henry Grinnell took an interest in Lorenzo's cause and search for his sisters. Grinnell was a private citizen who never stopped helping Lorenzo from 1853 until Olive was rescued. He organized search parties and expeditions to search for any leads that might lead back to the Oatman sisters, generously helping Lorenzo with all his resources. While he was in Los Angeles, Lorenzo joined a gold-digging expedition in the mountains, hoping to make a living for himself while also looking for any new information that might lead him to his sisters. And it actually happened. The expedition heard rumors that one of the Oatman sisters still survives and currently lived with an unknown tribe, while the other had died in captivity.

This was enough to get things moving. Petitions and letters were sent to government officials and military generals, and Lorenzo hoped that these rumors would be enough for the officials to take serious steps to find his last remaining sibling. The government moved and sent runners across the lands with messages to the indigenous people, and it finally paid off. They received information that there was a white woman living with the Mohave, and she was probably Olive, though they identified her as Spantsa.

A Quechan (Yuma Indian) tribesman called Francisco offered his help and to play messenger in the upcoming negotiations. Olive was about 19 years old when the messenger appeared, presumably in 1856. Francisco delivered the letter from Fort Yuma, in which officials asked for the return of the white girl that has been living with the Mohave, or at least to know the reason why she had not chosen to return thus far. The Mohave had no intention of returning Olive at first. They instead hid her and fought against the American demands. They even claimed that Olive was not white.

It is said that over the course of the negotiations, some of the Mohave expressed love and appreciation for

Olive, while others feared reprisal from the whites because they kept a white girl with them for years. It makes sense that the Indians had conflicting feelings about that Oatman girl. After all, she had been living with them for years now and had been fully integrated into the village life. Their fear of reprisal was also quite reasonable. The Americans were known for their violent, and often non-proportional, attacks whenever one of their own was harmed by the Indians.

Francisco halted negotiations for a while and rested in some Mohave homes. Shortly after, he persisted and tried to convince the tribe to let Olive go for everyone's sake. This second time around, he began trading. He offered them a white horse (which sweetened the deal greatly) and blankets, as well as other things that the Mohave often needed. Francisco was also clear in his message that the whites would attack and destroy the Mohave if Olive was not returned. The negotiations were relentless, and they lasted for three days. The tribal leaders of the Mohave wanted to keep Olive for more reasons than one, especially as an advantage to maintain friendly relations with the American military, which could be more useful than letting her go.

Eventually, the chief and the elders agreed to let Olive go after some discussions among the Mohave, and it is said that Olive herself was a part of these discussions, which goes to show how highly the tribe thought of her. And thus, Olive Oatman was released, and she traveled back to Fort Yuma. She was accompanied by Topeka, Aespaneo's daughter, who often took care of Olive during her time with the Mohave. The trip took 20 long days, during which Olive was conflicted about this new chapter of her life.

Olive was dressed in traditional tribal attire on her journey, a willow bark dress. She was then given a dress by one of the army officer's wives so she would be 'properly presentable' before arriving since the Indian outfits were considered too revealing for the westerns. Olive was given a hero's welcome as soon as she stepped into the fort, cheered by the people and celebrated. The Olive Oatman that returned to Fort Yuma was not the same one that had left years earlier with her family in an attempt to find the holy city of Bashan. It is said that Olive had almost forgotten the English language after years of not speaking it. She stuttered and struggled to speak in her native tongue. It took her a while until she grew reaccustomed to the language she had grown up speaking. Her skin was darker, too, by years of hard work in the scorching sun.

Most of all, she had a blue too on her chin, which was unmistakably the first thing that people noticed upon looking at her. Olive Oatman was cared for by the women in the Fort, and they looked after her until her English slowly improved and she regained familiarity with American customs.

It is said that Olive Oatman covered her face and wept when she was delivered to the Americans in Fort Yuma. Some even described her as a grieving woman who mourned the loss of the tribal life that she had known for several years. This is why her childhood friend, whom Olive later befriended again, Susan Thompson, said that she believed that Olive lamented the family she left behind, which was denied by Olive, as we mentioned earlier.

A few days into her stay at Fort Yuma; Olive began speaking a few English words. She soon found out that her brother Lorenzo was alive and had spent years looking for her and Mary Ann. Lorenzo, too, learned about Olive's ransom, and he instantly left his home in California and traveled to be reunited with his sister. Their reunion made headline news and was widely covered (and celebrated) at the time.

Lorenzo came to Fort Yuma to accompany his sister back to Los Angeles, where she could start leading some semblance of a normal life. Upon leaving Fort Yuma, this was the last time it is believed that Olive saw someone of her Mohave family. The tribe member greeted her and Lorenzo as they were leaving the fort by wagon. It is said that Olive replied to the greeting and told the Mohave in his native tongue, *"I will tell all about the Mohave and how I lived with them. Good-bye."* Olive left the Fort with her brother, leaving the Mohave tribe behind and carrying her time with them as a memory that would accompany her until her death.

Olive Oatman was not the first white to be kidnapped by the Indians to be ransomed later, and she would not be the last. Such incidents were quite common in those centuries. In many cases, the Indians would adopt some of the prisoners into their tribal life and accept them as one of their own. These are some other similar incidents to Olive's. Some of the captives in these stories were ransomed and managed to gradually return to the white community, albeit with some difficulty. Others spent their entire lives with the Indians and died with them.

The Johnson Family is one such example. The French and Indian war lasted from 1754 to 1763, and it saw the colonies of British America clash with those of New

France. Each colonist side had tribal natives fighting alongside their forces, which resulted in several terrible battles over the long war. There were also several instances of kidnapping and ransoming of settlers, like that which happened to Susannah Willard Johnson and her family.

Susannah Johnson was born in Massachusetts in 1730 to a lineage of puritan settlers in New England. In the year 1747, she got married to James Johnson in her hometown, and they had seven children together. The tensions between the French and the British caught up with many during those turbulent years, including the Johnsons. By 1749, the Johnson family settled in Fort no. 4 in New Hampshire. That year saw a fickle peace between the French and the British, and by 1753, there were rarely attacks on the town of fort no. 4, so things were relatively calm. One year later, however, as the French and British tensions escalated again, rumors of an impending war grew.

The colonists in the area began panicking at the premise of new raids by the Indians, but Captain James Johnson eased their worries upon returning from a trading trip by late 1754. He told them that he was told on his journey that the war would not erupt until the following year, which put people's minds at rest for a while. The people believed that they would have time to relocate out of the fort and to a safer part of New Hampshire. The Johnsons even hosted a dinner party for their neighbors on August 29 to celebrate the good news. Unfortunately, they did not know what the next few hours would have in store for them.

It was the early hours of the morning of August 30 when the attack happened. Like most of the township, the Johnsons were asleep. A war party of Abenaki Indians raided Fort no.4. They ended up kidnapping Susannah and her husband, as well as their three children: a boy, 6 years old, called Sylvanus, and the sisters Polly and Susanna, 2 and 4, respectively. They also took Susannah Johnson's 14 years old sister, Miriam Willard. The Abenaki also took the Johnsons' neighbors, Peter Labarree and his hired servant called Ebenezer Farnsworth. After looting the family house, the Indians burned the Johnson family home.

This was a terrible time for such a kidnapping as Susannah was in the last month of her pregnancy. The next day, as they were trekking the trail with the Indians, Susannah gave birth to a girl whom she named Elizabeth Captive. The road was grueling for the family, especially after Susannah gave birth. Food had also run out during their journey, so a horse they had was killed and eaten so that the party would not starve to death. The Indians took their prisoner to their village, Saint-François-du-Lac. The Johnsons thought that they would be slaughtered after their three-week-long journey. This fear was amplified when the prisoners were forced to 'run the gauntlet' with rows of Abenaki warriors on either side, armed with tomahawks and clubs.

Susannah later wrote in her journal that she was *"agreeably disappointed"* when the Indians did not beat them to death but rather, *"each Indian only gave us a tap on the shoulder."* She also noted that the natives were especially 'decent' with the women, and none were harmed. The Johnsons spent two to three months in captivity, during which they were starting to actually develop some Abenaki vocabulary and accustom themselves to the tribal life. Sadly, this new life did not last for too long. It was common back then for captives to be taken to Montreal, where they would be ransomed. The Indians started with James Johnson and his two oldest daughters. The rest of the Johnsons' neighbors were then taken one by one to Montreal, where they would be sold or ransomed.

In late October, Susannah and her son Sylvanus and infant daughter Elizabeth were the only captives remaining with the Abenaki. By November, Susannah and her daughter were sold to a French family and ended up in Montreal eventually. In Montreal, they were reunited with the rest of the family after being delivered to the merchant René de Couagne. Sylvanus, however, was adopted into the tribe and was prevented from leaving. James was finally given a two-month leave so he could travel to Massachusetts or New York to gather funds to ransom his entire family. He returned in 1755 without any money, and as such, he and his wife, along with Polly and Elizabeth, were sent to jail, while little Susanna was left in the care of "three affluent old maids," so she did not spend any jail time.

The Johnsons' "conditions were too shocking for description," and the entire family got smallpox. They spent two years in jail, from July 1755 to June 1757, with six months of those in a criminal jail and the rest in a civil one. In the last month of 1756, Susannah gave birth to a boy who died a few hours later. Susannah had petitioned the governor for the release of her family after spending over two years in jail. By the end of June 1757, she received a letter that her pleas were successful, and her family would be exchanged for French prisoners and sent to England. Unfortunately, this pardon did not include the husband and father. James Johnson remained in prison to complete his sentence. Susannah and her girls (except for Susanna), along with her sister Miriam (who rejoined the family at some point), returned to England while James stayed behind.

The Johnson family returned to North America after James was released so they could be reunited with him. It was, however, to be short-lived. James died in 1758 in the Battle of Ticonderoga. Sylvanus was six years old at the time of the raid and his abduction. He was adopted into the Abenaki and was finally returned to his family in 1759 after being ransomed for five hundred lives. Accounts from that time report that Sylvanus, 11 upon reuniting with his family, was all but Indian. He had completely forgotten English by then and was, instead, fluent in Abenaki as well as French. The boy gradually, and slowly, reassimilated into the English white community, but it is said that he retained some Abenaki customs and traditions until he died.

Finally, a year or so later, at the end of 1760, Susanna (the oldest Johnson daughter) was returned to her family after the French gave up Montreal. She had spent all this time with a French catholic family in Montreal. Upon her return, she spoke only French.

Susannah Johnson eventually remarried and had seven more children. Forty years after her capture, in 1796, she decided to tell the story of her captivity by the Indians, and the ordeal that her family had gone through, which left them all changed until they died. She used any letters that survived those years, journals, and testimonies from her family and neighbors, who were eventually returned. She eventually went on to publish several editions about her captivity by the Indians, and after some revisions and additions over the years, her accounts are all highly regarded and read to this day. At that time, Indian captivity stories were a genre of their own, with many books and volumes telling different tales, but Susannah Johnson's account remains one of the most riveting and accurate depictions of this experience and what it was truly like. The story was republished many times after her death and is still studied until now.

Mary Jemison's story is one of the most famous in the lore of captivity narrative. This story is uniquely different than all others because Jemison not only chose to stay with the Indians, but she also married within that tribal community, not once, but twice. She also had children with her husbands.

Mary Jemison was born on a ship headed from Ireland to America in 1743. The ship landed in Philadelphia, Pennsylvania, and the family was joined by other Scotch-Irish immigrants that were flooding into the new world. Her parents had a few other children over the upcoming few years, but things were about to take a bad turn for the family. They were also affected by the French and Indian war. As we mentioned earlier, native Indians were used heavily in this war on both sides.

The dates vary in regard to when Mary Jemison was abducted. Some put it at 1755, while others put the date at 1758. The story goes that one morning, a party of six Shawnee Indians and French soldiers attacked the family farm. Mary was 12 or 15 by then, and she was taken by the marauders along with her family members, except for her two brothers, who managed to escape. Another young boy from another family was taken prisoner as well. On the road to the French fort, Mary's family was killed by the Shawnee and scalped in an Indian ritual. They killed her parents and siblings, sparing Mary and the young boy with her.

"On our march that day, an Indian went behind us with a whip, with which he frequently lashed the children, to make them keep up. In this manner, we

traveled till dark, without a mouthful of food or a drop of water, although we had not eaten since the night before. Whenever the little children cried for water, the Indians would make them drink urine or go thirsty. At night they encamped in the woods, without fire and without shelter, where we were watched with the greatest vigilance. Extremely fatigued and very hungry, we were compelled to lie upon the ground without supper or a drop of water to satisfy the cravings of our appetites. As in the daytime, so the little ones were made to drink urine in the night if they cried for water. Fatigue alone brought us a little sleep for the refreshment of our weary limbs, and at the dawn of day, we were again started on our march, in the same order that we had proceeded the day before," Mary later said of her capture.

Mary also recounted that she and the young boy that was with her were taken away until the gruesome crime of killing her family was finished. She says, *"The Indian led us some distance into the bushes or woods, and there lay down with us to spend the night. The recollection of parting with my tender mother kept me awake while the tears constantly flowed from my eyes. A number of times in the night, the little boy begged of me earnestly to run away with him and get clear of the Indians; but remembering the advice I had so lately received, and knowing the dangers to which we should be exposed, in traveling without a path and without a guide, through a wilderness unknown to us, I told him that I would not go, and persuaded him to lie still till morning.*

My suspicion as to the fate of my parents proved too true, for soon after I left them, they were viciously tomahawked to death and scalped, together with Robert, Matthew, Betsey, and the woman and her two children, and mangled in the most shocking manner."

The ritual turned out to be, as Mary later found out, a tradition among Iroquoians-speaking peoples that was done to mourn and avenge their fallen. When one of their own was killed in battle or even taken as a prisoner, they demanded scalps from an enemy prisoner in what is considered a mourning ritual, brutal as it might seem. This ritual was done to avenge the death of a tribesman who died earlier in the war. . The Shawnee had intended to kidnap prisoners and get their scalps as compensation for that loss, and so they did. Mary and the young boy were spared because they were of adoption age, as most historians agree.

Mary also recalled seeing the Indians take some of the scalps (including her family's) one night by the fire and started preparing them for the market. They did so by "*straining them over small hoops which they prepared for that purpose, and then drying and scraping them by the fire. Having put the scalps, yet wet and bloody, upon the hoops, and stretched them to their full extent, they held them to the fire till they were partly dried, and then, with their knives, commenced scraping off the flesh; and in that way, they continued to work, alternately drying and scraping them, till they were dry and clean. That being done, they combed the hair in the neatest manner and then painted it and the edges of the scalps, yet on the hoops, red.*"

Mary also recalled seeing the familiar color of her family scalps, including her mother's red hair.

Upon reaching the French fort, Mary was taken in by two Seneca women who in turn accompanied Mary to their nearby settlement. In the natives' village, Mary was adopted into a Seneca family after a brief ceremony. She was renamed Dehgewanus, or some other variant of the word, which translated to a beautiful girl or pleasant thing, among other nice translations. And thus, Mary's new life among the Seneca began.

She spent the next few years growing accustomed to the natives' lifestyle and learning their habits. Upon reaching the age of marriage, Mary got married to a

Delaware native called Sheninjee, who had been living with the Seneca. She gave birth to a girl in mid-1761, but the girl died soon after birth. Not shortly after, Mary gave birth to a son that they named Thomas in honor of her father, whom Mary missed dearly.

Sheninjee soon worried that the end of the war might mean the return of all captives, and he worried that he would lose his wife. So, he decided to take his small family and embark on a long journey to his homeland to prevent that from happening. He took Mary and young Thomas on a 700-mile journey to Sehgahunda Valley, today's Western New York, along the Genesee River.

It was a grueling journey in extreme weather conditions at times, and unfortunately, the husband did not survive. Mary, now Dehgewanus, lost her husband when he left them to go hunting and ended up falling ill and dying on the road to his native home. Mary reached the Sehgahunda Valley with young Thomas. She was now a widow arriving in a new land with no friends or family but her infant son. Fortunately, Sheninjee's clan relatives were kind to her, and they made a home for Mary in Little Beard's town, not far from present time's Cuylerville, New York.

Life was kind to Mary, and she ended up remarrying a Seneca by the name Hiakatoo. Mary gave birth to six children from Hiakatoo. This was a time she looked fondly back on and described it as a time where she and her adopted people lived peacefully and happily. Unfortunately, the peace was not to last for long. The American Revolutionary War started in 1775, and it ushered with it a new wave of violence that would affect the Seneca and Mary. The Seneca sided with the British in the hopes that the British triumphing would help the natives get rid of the relentless colonials and the trouble that comes with them. In allying themselves with the British, the Seneca and other native tribes on the British side became a target for the American army. This was a troubling time for the Seneca, Mary included, and she recounted that period and her own efforts in helping native Indians against the rebel colonists.

By 1779, the Seneca had become a nuisance for the American army, so George Washington decided to destroy their will and ability to fight. He sent an army of five thousand strong, and their attack was focused on Little Beard's Town. The Seneca tried to ambush the invading Americans, but it was to no avail. The Americans did suffer some significant losses, but they managed to push forward and reached the Genesee

Valley, and the onslaught began. The Americans burned the villagers' homes and their fields, adamant about destroying Seneca's ability to fight any longer in the future.

The Seneca knew that the American army was approaching Little Beard's Town, and death would befall any Indians who crossed their path. So, they fled the town into the woodlands. Some made for distant Seneca villages that were not a target of the Americans. Mary decided to head to an abandoned village south of Little Beard's called Gadaho. She took her family there, and she spent the next sixty years or so of her life in Gadaho. Things were peaceful in that once abandoned village, and Mary and her children were taken in by two fleeing slaves. She returned to the Seneca ways in that village, and it is believed that she was reunited with her husband, Hiakatoo. For two decades, things were peaceful, and the family enjoyed a relatively calm life.

However, this peace was also ephemeral. More invaders came to the Seneca towns and villages, but this time they were not soldiers. They were land settlers who were looking for new places for their expansion. This happened because the British gave up all lands east of the Mississippi River to the Americans without consulting or discussing it with their native Indian allies. The Seneca held a council of elders and women who would advise the elders to discuss this new doom. Mary was a part of these negotiations, and it is said that she was a skilled one, too. She was able to improve the terms of the deal that forced the Seneca to give up their lands to the Americans. All in all, though, the deal was not good, and many Seneca did not approve of it. They eventually were forced to give up their lands to the Americans in 1797.

Things were gradually becoming much worse for the Seneca, and their lives were constantly affected by the growing white influence across their lands and territories. Sadly, for Mary's family, the constantly changing and troubling circumstances took a toll on her children, and three of them died in the span of six years. Her son, John, killed his brother Jesse, and John was killed later on, and she lost another of her children during the period between 1811 and 1817.

As for Mary, she was highly respected among the Seneca. Known as the "White Woman of the Genesee," it was said that no one in need was turned from her door. At some point in her later years, Mary told her story to a minister, who wrote it down and published the story of Mary Jemison as we know it today. Like with Olive Oatman's story, some say that the minister's own beliefs affected his retelling of Mary's story. Many historians, however, believe that it was fairly accurate and showed that Mary did prefer life with the Seneca than what she had known to be the average life of a British colonial woman.

By 1823, the Seneca had sold most of their lands to the Americans but for a 2-acre land that was left for Mary Jemison to use, which she sold by 1831. She then moved to Buffalo Creek Reservation, where it was believed that some Seneca lived. She died in 1833, a Seneca.

Cynthia Ann Parker's is quite similar to Mary Jemison's in that she too was taken as a child and stayed with her captors. Parker's story, however, had a twist that made it even more complicated. Some even believe that she was the most famous captive of the Indians in all US history.

Born in 1825 (or 1827 in some sources) in Illinois, Cynthia's family moved to Texas around 1833. Her grandfather, John Parker, was hired to build a fort that could withstand the continuous raids by the Comanche Indians, which had been a nightmare for colonist expansion into Texas. So, he took his entire family there to work on this significant project. The Parker family got to work and built fortified blockhouses as well as what was later known as Fort Parker, a citadel.

In 1836, a war party of anything between 100 and 600 Comanche Indians attacked the unsuspecting community, and they inflicted significant losses to the Americans. John Parker and the men who were with him were few, and they were ill-prepared to fight against the fierce Comanche Indians, who were far more experienced when it came to warfare. During the attack, several captives were taken, including Cynthia Parker, who was either 8 or 11 at that time, according to different sources. Cynthia would go on to spend the next 24 years with the Indians, marrying one from among them as well.

Like many captives in her position, Cynthia was quickly integrated into the Comanche lifestyle and was adopted by a Tenowish Comanche couple who were kind to her and raised her as their own. Cynthia quickly forgot about her culture and became a fully assimilated Comanche. She became so integrated into her new society that she married a chieftain, Peta Nocona. Cynthia led a happy life with her husband, and she bore him three children, including the last free Comanche chief, Quanah Parker. Cynthia's husband loved her so much that he did not follow his tribe's culture that dictated the chieftains take several wives, and he remained loyally married to Cynthia.

It is said that several white traders and soldiers spotted Cynthia Parker several times over the years, but she had no desire to leave her Comanche family. She did not know, though, that her family never gave up hope on her return, especially her father, who often collaborated with Texas Rangers to try and find the missing Cynthia, who regularly sent search scouts. In 1860, a surprise raid by the rangers on the Comanche village saw Parker captured.

Cynthia's husband, Nocona, was believed to have been killed in the attack, though sources vary on this one, and she too would have most likely been shot had she not identified herself in broken English. The Rangers abducted Cynthia and her infant child. Upon returning to the white community, Cynthia Parker struggled to readjust, and she missed her native American family. She also missed her two sons greatly and often worried about them since she was just taken with her infant daughter.

Much media attention was given to Cynthia's story, which captivated the entire country. Returning after this many years made her a hero in many eyes, regardless of her own feelings. In 1861, she was even given over 4,000 acres and an annual pension. None of these things, though, managed to make Cynthia happy. Some sources claim that she tried to escape several times over the years with her daughter to return to the Comanche, and she was not comfortable or pleased in her new life. After over two decades with the Indians, this was the life that she had grown accustomed to. She could also never adjust to the attention that her story garnered. In 1862, her brother was appointed her guardian.

Things got much worse for Cynthia when her daughter died of pneumonia in 1864. This was the only child she still had contact with, who was also the last connection to her past life with the Comanche. After her daughter's death, Cynthia closed off to the world and was taken with grief. She refused to eat and to drink in many cases. She did not take to any words of solace or encouragement given to her by her relatives. A few years later, she died in her sister's home, unable to bear life without any of her children.

Her son, Quanah, is considered to be among the most important of the Comanche leaders. He moved her body to Post Oak Mission Cemetery in 1910, and he was buried next to her in 1911. In 1957, both their remains were taken to Fort Sill, Oklahoma.

Cynthia Parker's story is, yet another of a captive young girl who grew among the native Indians and became accustomed to their way of life. In a way, she was not much different from Olive Oatman. She, too, was unhappy in her renewed life back with the whites and struggled to adapt after many years among the Comanche as one of their own. What made things worse for Cynthia, though, was that she was separated from her children, never to see them again. Cynthia's story, however, goes to show what might have been. Her son, the son of a white woman of western descent, grew to become the most important Comanche chieftain of his time and what many consider to be the last free one.

This makes you wonder about how things could have gone had the colonists tried to peacefully mingle with the native Indians. Had the colonists truly wanted to make peace, such unions between whites and Indians would not have been forbidden and frowned upon by the whites as they were then. Relationships between communities could have prospered. Sadly, this was not the way things went down. Instead, those who were integrated into Indian communities were taken against their will, and in many cases, their families were killed. While the captives did grow to love and feel familiar in their new surroundings, but in several cases, like

Cynthia's, they ended up being ransomed or captured against their will, back into their white communities.

You can't help but feel sorry upon reading such instances where someone was snatched from their families as children to grow up among foreign communities. After growing accustomed to their new and different lives, many of those would be returned to their white communities once again. This created a significant identity struggle and left an everlasting mark on those who were unfortunate enough to suffer this fate. There are countless captivity stories, so many that it became a literary genre as mentioned. Many of the stories were published and republished, and many have been turned into operas, musicals, films, TV shows, and countless other media.

While those creative endeavors often tried to thrust us into these captivating, if usually horrifying, stories, none could really tell us how the likes of Cynthia Parker of Olive Oatman felt. You have testimonies and opinions from that era, but how can we be certain that this is how these girls truly felt. As you will see in this upcoming chapter, life after returning from captivity was difficult for Olive Oatman, and she never really readjusted. Many of those women who were taken captive, whether they returned or spent their lives with the Indians, never really knew peace throughout their lives. It was in death that they finally rested.

CHAPTER SIX

~

A New Life

After Lorenzo took Olive and returned to Los Angeles, things were much different for her from the tribal life she had grown accustomed to. Olive Oatman's story was sought after by every major newspaper in the west, and she shared it with those who would listen. Many people were curious to learn about her life and the years that she spent in captivity, and what life was like with Indians. The narrative that was constantly fed to the colonists was that Indians were savage people who were ruthless and inferior to the white man. Seeing one who had lived much of her life with the Indians, the people were naturally curious to hear Olive's story, and they were riveted by it.

As we mentioned earlier, Olive Oatman then started a lecture circuit across the west to share her story with the world. This was when she got to know the Reverend Stratton, who authored the semi-fictional retelling of Olive Oatman's tale of captivity. The book became a hit and became one of the bestsellers of that time, selling 30,000 copies to the masses that were both fascinated and terrified by encounters with native Indians. With the book turning in a decent profit, Stratton used the royalties to give Olive and Lorenzo an education. They both attended the University of the Pacific.

Olive and Lorenzo Oatman also went on a book tour across the country to promote the book and gave lectures in several book circuits. The people were particularly fascinated by Olive's story because looking upon her tattooed chin; you could tell that hers was not the average captivity story. People came from all over just to look at Olive and see the blue tattoo on her chin for themselves. Olive Oatman was considered the first tattooed American woman, and she was also one of the few (and first) female public speakers at that time. Some believe that Olive Oatman had a significant impact on the feminist movement, which was in its early stages. Her giving lectures and being in the public eye, a strong woman who survived a terrible ordeal, certainly lent to help perceive women in a different light than the common back then.

In late 1865, Olive Oatman was giving a lecture in Michigan with Stratton. It was there that she met a wealthy cattle baron called John B. Fairchild, and he was captivated by her. Fairchild himself had lost his brother in an attack by Indians about 11 years earlier in a cattle drive in Arizona. This was around the same time that Olive had been living with the Mohave. Olive married John, and he protected her for the rest of her life from the scrutiny and curiosity of the public eye, which was grueling at some point for Olive.

It is said that Stratton was not invited to the wedding, and he and Olive never met again—mostly because Olive did not reach out to the Reverend. Olive and her husband then moved to Sherman, Texas, where they lived peacefully and quietly. Texas was an excellent prospect for a clever businessman like Fairchild, and he garnered much success there, turning from a cattle baron to a banker. Fairchild founded the City Bank of Sherman. He bought a large Victorian mansion for his wife, and they lived there away from the public eye.

Olive's life upon returning from her time with the Mohave was anything but easy. Rumors chased her, and people looked at her differently. She was quite literally marked for life from her captivity, and there was no changing that. Being a household name had its consequences, and Olive struggled with her fame. The rumors had even started before she eventually returned.

The Los Angeles Star reported in 1856 (a month before Olive even returned) that she and her sisters were alive and were discovered, and both of them were married to Mohave chiefs. During her later lectures, Olive constantly denied having any Indian lovers or husbands. Unfortunately, this was a rumor that would follow her for many years.

It is highly agreed upon that Olive was unhappy in the years that followed, and her life was marred by her turbulent past. Some historians believed that she suffered from chronic post-traumatic stress for most of her life upon returning to the white community. Olive tried to find happiness in any way that she could, but it was never an easy thing to do. She even adopted a child with Fairchild a few years after their marriage. The baby girl, Mary Elizabeth (nicknamed Mamie), did not fill Olive's life with enough happiness and joy for her to overcome the troubling events of her past and the incessant feeling of not belonging.

Olive Oatman kept battling depression, and chronic headaches, for many decades to come. She rarely left her home, and when she did, she had to put on a veil to avoid the gazes of strangers in the street, who most likely would have identified her. Sometimes, she also put makeup on to cover the tattoo on her chin. Around

1881, it is believed that Olive spent a few months in a medical spa in Canada, mostly bed-ridden, because of her depression and fatigue.

Olive grew particularly interested in charity work in the latter part of her life. She was especially keen on helping a young orphanage, unsurprisingly. Due to her own plight, Olive was often sympathetic with orphans and the turmoil they go through. Some believe that Fairchild spent years tracking down copies of Stratton's book to burn them down, possibly in an attempt to erase all recorded history of his wife's time with the Indians and the ordeal she had gone through. With a story this highly publicized and renowned across the entire country, it was impossible to erase it from memory. Her story survived to this very day and is often mentioned when tales of captivity are broached.

It was rumored that Olive Oatman died in a mental asylum in New York State, but that is not true. It was actually the Reverend Stratton who was put in a mental asylum after he had fallen to hereditary insanity. He died shortly after being institutionalized. Before we get to Olive Oatman's death, let's jump back to Lorenzo. Her brother struggled over the years in search of wealth and success, but that was not an easy thing to do at that time. Lorenzo Oatman died at the age of 65 or so, and his lone sibling would soon follow.

About a year and a half later, Olive Oatman Fairchild died on March 20, 1903. She was in her mid-sixties, and she died of a heart attack. Olive Oatman was buried in West Hill Cemetery in Sherman, Texas, next to her loving husband. Olive's death ended the tale of a young girl who had lost her entire family in a brutal war that saw many lives destroyed.

There is no denying that Olive Oatman led what many would have considered a great life after returning from captivity with the Indians. She was married to a wealthy man who loved her, and everything she wanted was within reach. Yet, she could never fully adapt to this new life, despite having everything she wanted. Olive Oatman might have lost her mother at a very young age, brutally slaughtered at the hands of a ruthless marauding party. Yet, Olive had another mother. So she most likely lamented the loss of the Mohave family that she grew to love and appreciate, despite everything.

Aespaneo, Olive's adoptive Mohave mother, loved Olive and Mary Ann as her own children. Olive recalled that Aespaneo "*wept and wept from the heart and aloud . . . for a whole night,*" when Mary Ann lay dying from the famine that killed many Indians that time. Olive also often spoke fondly of her adoptive Mohave mother, who saved her life in more ways than one. *"Had it not been for her,"* Olive later said about Aespaneo, *"I might have perished."* And it was true. As we mentioned earlier, Aespaneo smuggled food to Olive in a time where there was none, and many died because of that famine. This goes to show just how much Aespaneo loved the Oatman sisters. It was Aespaneo who also accepted Olive's pleas to bury Mary Ann rather than cremate her, which was the Mohave tradition. It is even said that the Mohave matriarch insisted that her husband produces two of the tribe's best blankets just to wrap Mary Ann for her final rest!

This also makes Olive's return even more terrible, if you think about it. Olive Oatman lost two mothers over the course of a few decades. The first, her biological mother, was slaughtered by a raiding party. Then, after Olive had grown to love and appreciate another motherly figure in Aespaneo, she was again snatched from her mother, never to see her again. One can only imagine what such a terrible loss could to a person, but it certainly was quite difficult for Olive. She missed her Mohave family, and it showed. Her depression in later life and general unhappiness were because she had come to think of herself as one of the tribe, as did those who first saw her upon her return. The commander at Fort Yuma did not believe that Olive was a white woman at first. They had to pull back her hair and show that behind her ears was white, just to convince him that she was indeed not an Indian. This is how much assimilated Olive Oatman had become.

It is even said that Lorenzo did not recognize Olive after he first met her. Some say they embraced and wept into each other's arms. Other versions of the story claim that they both sat in a room for an hour, saying nothing. Lorenzo was so taken back by her transformation; he was at a loss for words. Was it possible that part of Olive's transformation and unhappiness upon return was because she did indeed have a family with the Mohave? There are some who think so. It is unlikely, but definitely not impossible. Some claim that Olive's adoptive mother, Aespaneo, raised her children when she was taken away to return to the white community. If that was the case, then Olive's depression would definitely make a lot of sense. Sadly, we might never know the truth about her true relationships with the Mohave.

A potential family aside, Olive had grown to love the place. The native Indians of that time led exotic lives, surrounded by nature from all directions. It was a beautiful and relaxing life, which was unlike the traditional life for a woman in the colonies. *"I could not leave the wild mountain home without a struggle,"* Olive wrote about her time while considering leaving the Mohave to rejoin the white community. *"Every stream and mountain park and shaded glen I was as familiar with, as with the dooryard of my childhood home. Those grand old solitudes possessed a peculiar charm for me."*

As you can see from this quote, Olive did like being with the Mohave. Her affection for them was so genuine and tangible; many people refused the accounts from her lectures and the book published by Stratton, which (despite its general anti-Indian narrative) could not hide Olive Oatman's affection for the Mohave and her time with them. People were so incredulous about Olive's experience and her fondness of the Mohave; they instead chose to believe that Olive must have been tortured, raped, starved, and most importantly, brainwashed to reach this point where she had actually grown fond of those who had captured her.

After her death, letters were found that showed just how much pain Olive was in. She suffered from the psychological trauma of her childhood until her death. This terrible stress and sadness could be because her family was slaughtered before her eyes. Yet, it could also be because Olive was wrenched away from her second family, the Mohave, whom she had come to love and respect.

One thing is for sure, though. Olive's life and the events that transpired in it affected all those who came in contact with her. Remember Francisco? He was the Indian who mediated Olive's release and negotiated with the Mohave for several days in order to secure her return. After his role in those events, Francisco was held in very high regard by the whites, who were grateful for his role in returning the Oatman girl. He was eventually made chief of his tribe by the Yuma and assumed his new role with significant arrogance and pride with his people, but he is said to have always been kind and acted differently with the whites.

Around 1857, the Mohave and the Yumas fought together against the Maricopas, which would soon bear an ill fate for Francisco. A large band of those two tribes attacked Maricopas villages. They killed left and right and burned houses, even slaughtering women and children in the process. This was an act of war that would not be taken lightly. The Maricopas and their allies, the Pimas and Papagoes, gathered a force that could match that of the Yumas and Mohaves. The two forces clashed at Maricopa Wells, and a fierce battle took place there. The Yumas were defeated and lost hundreds of warriors in this great battle, and it is said that only three returned alive.

In this battle, Francisco was killed. It is believed, however, that he was killed by his own men. This was because many of his men believed that Francisco had brought this chaos and carnage upon them when he helped and defended the whites. Thus, the man who negotiated Olive Oatman's return was killed for his efforts by those who were loyal to him, according to tales from that period.

CONCLUSION

Olive Oatman's legacy endures to this very day. The town of Oatman in Arizona was named after her family and is now a tourist stop, where people come to hear the stories about one of the most famous American captives in history. Another historic town named after her is Olive City, Arizona. It was a steamboat stop back during the gold rush years, and it was renamed in Olive Oatman's honor. There are also several other places named after her, including the Oatman Flat (where the family was murdered and Olive and her sister abducted), Oatman Flat Station, and Oatman Mountain.

The remains of the family are an enduring and horrible legacy to this very day due to that fateful decision Royce Oatman made a long time ago. As mentioned earlier, the remains were transferred several times, first to move from the cairn to a more permanent resting place deep in the soil, which was undone because of a flood. Eventually, the Daughters of the American Revolution gathered the massacred Oatman family remains and moved them to a more fitting granite and concrete memorial. It has a bronze plaque with the following words:

In Memory Of

The Oatman Family

Six Members Of This Pioneer Family

Massacred By Indians In March 1851

Erected By The Arizona Society

Daughters Of The American Revolution – 1954

Several books have been written about the Oatman family massacre and, in particular, Olive Oatman's abduction and consequent plight. She remains a lasting figure in literary history, and her story is still read to this very day. In television, Olive Oatman is paid homage in AMC's Hell on Wheels. The character Eva Oakes is loosely based on Olive Oatman. She, too, in the show, had a blue chin tattoo and was raised a Mormon. Olive Oatman's story was also hinted at in other shows, like The Ghost Inside My Child: The Wild West and Tribal Quest, where a character claimed that she was Olive Oatman reincarnated.

There were also five or six books published based on the Oatman family story, many of which became bestsellers of their era. The story of Olive Oatman's captivity was particularly fascinating for many people because she was the first white woman to be tattooed by a tribal tattoo, and she lived to tell the story and show her scars to the world.

Royce Oatman's decision to brave the dangers of the trail will live in infamy and will always be remembered when tales of native Indian violence are brought up. His stubbornness might have cost the family their lives, but it is not entirely his fault. Royce was kind to the Indian party, and he offered them as much food as he could spare. He didn't even protest when they ransacked his family's belonging. The violence that ensued against the Oatman family was unjustified and is a testament that oppression and tough living conditions can make people unpredictable and dangerously violent.

Olive Oatman's story will always be controversial and filled with different opinions and accounts. Contemporary retellings of her story paint the Indians as savages and claim that her time with them was filled with torture and slavery. Some will claim she forced into a marriage and bore Indian children.

Others will claim that she was happy with the Mohave, based on several pieces of evidence and through Olive's words herself when she spoke of her time in captivity, which quickly turned from a captive situation into one where she assimilated into her new community and even grew fond of it.

However, how you wish to view Olive Oatman's story is up to you. One could choose to believe that she was happy in her new life, and she did not want to leave and was burdened by sadness that she had to. Or you could choose to believe that Olive Oatman was unhappy with the Mohave and resented them and that the Indians were mean and cruel to her. Yet, Olive Oatman is much more than that. Her legacy is one that shows that what we perceive as boundaries of identity and race are unreliable and not necessarily true. Olive Oatman was proof that peaceful coexistence between white settlers and indigenous Plain Indians was possible had there been enough will and intention to walk that path.

Olive's story is one that shows that the Old West did not have to be this wild, and it did not need to carry this huge death toll. At the end of the day, the Americans and Indians learned to peacefully co-exist, but many were brutally slaughtered before reaching that. It's important that we learn about our history because those who don't read the past are doomed to repeat it. While captivity stories might not happen in this day and age, the racial tensions and corrupt souls that led to this story are still around hundreds of years later.

To this very day, some look upon other races and judge them to be inferior or 'subhuman' or 'savages' and other unpleasant labels. If there is one thing we should learn from Olive's story, it is that co-existing is possible between people who never thought it might be. Her tale of survival and then assimilation and growth goes to show us that violence is never the answer. Olive Oatman had to live with her scars, physical and spiritual, but she left an enduring legacy that should and has to lead to coexistence and homogeneity. Humanity would certainly be all the better for it.

Captivity stories are there for us to read and learn from. Incidents like Olive Oatman's should not have happened, but they did several times across history. Young children were taken from their parents and plucked away from the life they knew. However, before we jump into condemning the savages who committed such crimes, we need to look into the backstories of why these abductions happened in the first place. The history of the United States as a country is a complicated one, and it is filled with a lot of controversies, enough to fill hundreds of books. It is important, though, to look upon such events through an objective lens because we stand to gain much from stories like Olive Oatman's even today.

Thank you for Reading, if you enjoyed the book I would appreciate a review on amazon, thank you.

Niall

REFERENCES

Bair, J. (2019, March 28). Our Turn At This Earth: A plains state without Indians. Retrieved from Hppr.org website: https://www.hppr.org/post/our-turn-earth-plains-state-without-indians-0

The culture of violence in the American West: Myth versus reality. (n.d.). Retrieved from Independent.org website: https://www.independent.org/publications/tir/article.asp?id=803

The Abduction of Olive Oatman. (n.d.). Retrieved from Womenshistory.org website: https://www.womenshistory.org/articles/abduction-olive-oatman

Oatman Massacre and Captivity of the Oatman Sisters, as related to J. Ross Browne in 1864. (n.d.). Retrieved from Carlsbadhistoricalsociety.com website: https://www.carlsbadhistoricalsociety.com/Carlsbad%20Historical%20Society_files/historical/Oatman%20Massacre.htm

Prisoners, students, and thinkers: Susannah Willard Johnson. (2015, June 19). Retrieved from Morrin.org website: https://www.morrin.org/en/publications-de-la-lhsq/prisoners-students-and-thinkers/prisonniers-eleves-et-penseurs-susannah-willard-johnson/

(N.d.). Retrieved from Letchworthparkhistory.com website: http://www.letchworthparkhistory.com/jem.html

Deshields, J. T. (2008). Cynthia Ann Parker: The story of her capture at the massacre of the inmates of parker's fort. Alcester, England: Read Books.

Oatman Massacre and Captivity of the Oatman Sisters, as related to J. Ross Browne in 1864. (n.d.). Retrieved from Carlsbadhistoricalsociety.com website: https://www.carlsbadhistoricalsociety.com/Carlsbad%20Historic al%20Society_files/historical/Oatman%20Massacre.htm

Mifflin, M. (2009, August 1). 10 myths about Olive Oatman. Retrieved from Truewestmagazine.com website: https://truewestmagazine.com/10-myths-about-olive-oatman/

Bell, B. B. (2018, February 26). Heart gone wild - true west magazine. Retrieved from Truewestmagazine.com website: https://truewestmagazine.com/heart-gone-wild/

Rasmussen, C. (2000, July 16). Tale of kindness didn't fit notion of savage Indian. The Los Angeles Times. Retrieved from https://www.latimes.com/archives/la-xpm-2000-jul-16-me-53856-story.html

McGinty, B. (2005). The Oatman massacre: A tale of desert captivity and survival. Norman, OK: University of Oklahoma Press.

Van Huygen, M. (2015, November 16). Olive Oatman, the pioneer girl abducted by Native Americans who returned a marked woman. Retrieved from Mentalfloss.com website:

https://www.mentalfloss.com/article/81424/retrobituaries-olive-oatman-pioneer-girl-who-became-marked-woman

Macri, B. (2018, January 27). Oatman massacre: The bones still speak - an American stream. Retrieved from Anamericanstream.com website: https://anamericanstream.com/oatman-massacre-the-bones-still-speak/

Aron, S., Zocalo Public Square, & Stephen Aron, Z. P. S. (2016, August 16). The history of the American west gets a much-needed rewrite. Retrieved from Smithsonian Magazine website: https://www.smithsonianmag.com/history/history-american-west-gets-much-needed-rewrite-180960149/

How wild was the Wild West? (2019, July 1). Retrieved from Historyextra.com website: https://www.historyextra.com/period/victorian/wild-west-how-lawless-was-american-frontier/

The Lachine massacre. (n.d.). CBC News. Retrieved from https://www.cbc.ca/history/EPCONTENTSE1EP3CH1PA4LE.html

Guns germs & steel: Variables. Smallpox. (n.d.). Retrieved from Pbs.org website: https://www.pbs.org/gunsgermssteel/variables/smallpox.html

Kalinago genocide of Carib Indians. (n.d.). Retrieved from Candid.org website: https://nativephilanthropy.candid.org/events/kalinago-genocide-of-carib-indians/

Mark, J. J. (2021). Indian Massacre of 1622. World History Encyclopedia. Retrieved from https://www.ancient.eu/Indian_Massacre_of_1622/

Pre-revolution timeline 1600s, Detail 1655, peace tree war - America's Best History. (n.d.). Retrieved from Americasbesthistory.com website: https://americasbesthistory.com/abhtimeline1655m.html

Guertin, J. (2020, June 5). Nine Men's Misery. Retrieved from Newengland.com website: https://newengland.com/today/travel/rhode-island/nine-mens-misery-historic-site-in-cumberland-ri/

The Lachine massacre. (n.d.). CBC News. Retrieved from https://www.cbc.ca/history/EPCONTENTSE1EP3CH1PA4LE.html

Made in the USA
Coppell, TX
29 June 2021